THE MUSIC LOVER'S POETRY ANTHOLOGY

THE MUSIC LOVER'S POETRY ANTHOLOGY

Edited by **HELEN HANDLEY HOUGHTON**
and **MAUREEN MCCARTHY DRAPER**

A Karen & Michael Braziller Book
PERSEA BOOKS / NEW YORK

Persea Books, Inc.
853 Broadway
New York, NY 10003

Library of Congress Cataloging-in-Publication Data

The music lover's poetry anthology / edited by Helen Handley Houghton and Maureen McCarthy Draper ; foreword by J. D. McClatchy.
   p. cm.
ISBN 978-0-89255-333-4 (alk. paper)
1. Music—Poetry. 2. American poetry. 3. English poetry. I. Houghton, Helen Handley. II. Draper, Maureen McCarthy.
  PS595.M684M86 2007
  808.81'93578—dc22

         2006102261

Designed by Rita Lascaro

If I had my life to live over again, I would have made a rule to read some poetry and listen to some music at least once a week; for perhaps the parts of my brain now atrophied would have thus been kept active through use. The loss of these tastes is a loss of happiness, and may possibly be injurious to the intellect, and more probably to the moral character, by enfeebling the emotional part of our nature.　　　—CHARLES DARWIN

Contents

Horns, Woodwinds, & Strings

OPERA

JAZZ & BLUES

PERFORMANCES

Foreword

THERE HAVE BEEN SOME EXALTED CLAIMS made. Poetry, Paul Valéry insisted, isn't speech raised to the level of music, but music dragged down to the level of speech. Though Aristotle made metaphor rather than music the defining characteristic of a poem, most authorities have wanted to bind poetry's origins and emphasis to that of song—some sort of ritualized sound of exaltation or lamentation, a chant rising from the group but heard in the soul of each. If architecture too is "frozen music," it may be that all the arts want to have their birth in music, because none of them has—and all of them yearn for—music's uncanny power to enter a listener immediately and take entire control of his body and spirit. It is the most godly of the arts in its ability to take possession of us, literally to take us out of this world. We do not ask what the music means. We are the music.

Poetry, on the other hand, seems to have lowlier intentions. The word itself derives from the Greek *poiein*, to make or pile up, a process altogether more physical and willful than the sublime spontaneity we associate with music. Still, from the start, poetry has wanted to imitate music's rhythms of repetition and recurrence, its delicate harmonies, its expressive dissonances and silences. Elizabethan madrigals, the sweep of Shakespearean verse, the jeweled precisions of Pope's couplets, the plangent melancholy of Keats—in the best poetry we sense an instinctive control. In the texture of lines by Hopkins or Hart Crane, by Mallarmé or Leopardi, by Swinburne or Stevens, we can persuade ourselves that we actually hear a music, a lilt or electricity made by words but somehow beyond them. Poetry in the twentieth century deliberately drove itself away from music and towards speech as the source of its authority, and the resulting free verse is often flat, hesitant, nasal.

Notes express sound. Words express sound and meaning. At the right pitch, words can fulfill Ezra Pound's conviction that there exists "an 'absolute rhythm,' a rhythm, that is, in poetry which corresponds exactly to the emotion or shade of emotion to be expressed." But Pound's ideal is expressive, not musical. Music doesn't correspond to emotions, it creates patterns that may evoke emotions, and in doing so will always surpass the lumbering pace of language.

Still, we don't want just to experience pleasure; we want to remember it. We want to think about what cannot be readily articulated. We can only repeat the music, but we can read endlessly varying accounts of it, and one of poetry's triumphant achievements is to recall and celebrate. The poems in this book do just that. Occasionally they try to describe the sound of music, as when Lorca says that the guitar breaks the glasses of the dawn, or Jan Zwicky says of Bill Evans's piano that it "makes night fall around it / like the glow from a reading lamp." But more often, the poets describe the effect of music—as Tolstoy, rather than describe Anna Karenina's beauty, describes instead its effect on others. Again and again, the poets capture the human moment when, as music is being played, a sorrow is calmed or a love at last understood. As mysterious as its effects is its origin, and poets have always been drawn to meditate on their counterparts, the composers. There have been no poetic prodigies to equal a Mozart or Mendelssohn or Saint-Saëns whose genius sprang fully formed from their youth and calls into question the nature of art itself. There can be no surprise that we reach helplessly for words like "divine" or "miraculous" to explain it. And there have been few writers who struggled so titanically as Beethoven, whose work calls into question any artist's ambition. Around these enigmas the poets circle with a wary wonder. And then there is the voice. If it is the finest of all instruments, it is also the poet's emblem, Apollo's prayer or the call of Eurydice from the dark.

Nothing in my life has made me feel alternately more and less lonely than music. Nothing has made more sense or shown me the limits of mere sense. As a child, reluctantly practicing the piano, I glimpsed through the tedium a world I could make—and by error unmake—and I had a model for life. When I was in my twenties and seeing a psychoanalyst because that life had blurred, I would come home from the sessions puzzled or disappointed, and then play LPs of Richard Strauss's *Metamorphosen* and Arnold Schoenberg's *Verklärte Nacht* and feel that *now* I had been understood. I have at times felt I understood love—but more often in my seat at Carnegie Hall than in the arms of my beloved. I think of Pasternak's description of a concert: "The melodies, mingling with the tears, run straight along your nerves to your heart, and you weep not because you feel sad, but because the way to your heart has been found so unerringly and so shrewdly." None of this is right or fair, but that is the allure of music. Four decades later, I can look back at that child and at that young writer, and feel a wry gratitude, because I see the trail of crumbs, looking now like notes on a stave, leading chord by rest to the man I am now. As a poet and librettist, I have the privilege of giving words to music, giving a shape to scenes and melodies.

The poems in this remarkable anthology are each a memory. Or, it might be better to say, the account of an unforgettable moment. In ways both witty and poignant, they remind us, again and again, of how music has shown us to ourselves more accurately, and given us as well the eerie means to understand transcendence—to step out of our lives and look back at them.

Decades ago, reporting on a concert she had attended that featured chamber music by Franz Schubert, the novelist Sylvia Townsend Warner wrote to a friend: "It struck me, as I listened, that with Schubert one has, more than with any other composer, the sensation of holding the music in one's hand, feeling it flutter and burn and strive there, as though one were holding a wild bird." Think of the poems that follow as a pair of hands holding for a moment what burns and strives, something wild and free.

J. D. McClatchy

Introduction

THE MUSIC LOVER'S POETRY ANTHOLOGY is a labor of love between two longtime friends, both pianists and teachers, whose lives would be unimaginable without either poetry or music. Each poem included in it is about a memorable encounter with music—listening to it, making it, performing it—and about those indelible, transporting experiences that music generates or leads us to recall and relive. While there have been anthologies of musical poems inspired by specific genres of music—jazz poems, for example—to the best of our knowledge there has never been a book like this one in its breadth and its particular interest in poems that explicitly consider music as their muse.

We all ask so much of both music and poetry, to help us touch the intangible parts of reality, to shape our feelings, to return the past to us in a burnished, enlivened form—to commemorate, to console, and to celebrate. But why do so many poets choose to write about music? (We have been amazed by their numbers.) Perhaps it is because it is the only art more lyrical than poetry itself in delineating the secrets and movements of our inner lives. In his eloquent memoir, *Living with Music,* Ralph Ellison writes, "In the swift whirl of time music is a constant, reminding us of what we were and of that toward which we aspired. Art thou troubled? Music will not only calm, it will ennoble thee." These poems about music have indeed ennobled us: they have elevated our minds and spirits, they have moved us.

This book is divided into nine chapters. The poems in each compose their own inspired harmonies, though they also echo and reverberate across these groupings, striking here an over-tone, there an antiphonal response. We hope that readers will find a combination of time-tested favorites and delightful discoveries. With some exceptions (Emily Dickinson, Thomas

Hardy, and Charles Baudelaire, for example) we have focused on contemporary and near-contemporary poets from the twentieth and twenty-first centuries. Among those we have included are six Nobel Laureates (Seamus Heaney, Czeslaw Milosz, Eugenio Montale, Pablo Neruda, Wislawa Szymborska, and Derek Walcott) and numerous Pulitzer Prize winners; an array of dazzling, if less trumpeted talents; and a wonderful selection of poets—Bruce Bond, Bill Holm, Donald Justice, William Matthews, and others—who are or were skilled musicians. Whoever the poet, the poems included are ones that make our senses finer and our ears attuned to "keener sounds," in the words of Wallace Stevens. Collectively they demonstrate, as the composer Sergei Prokofiev once said, that "there is still so much to be said in C Major!"

We have chosen not to include Shakespeare's musical universe—a volume in itself—nor have we included poems whose primary ambition is to *reproduce* the effects of music, as opposed to writing *of* them. Whether or not a reader shares our passion for Western classical and jazz traditions, it is our hope that the poems we have selected will give hours of pleasure and delight, as they have given us, and that they will keep sounding in memory long after the book has been closed.

We are grateful to all of the poets in this anthology. We especially want to thank those poets, musicians, friends, and relations who offered suggestions and encouragement: Bascove, Jill Bialosky, Coleman Barks, Robert Bly, Bobbie Bristol, Don Campbell, Lyn Chase, Nicholas Christopher, Billy Collins, Judy Collins, Fred Courtright, Suzanne Doyle, Nancy Flowers, Jonathan Galassi, David Godine, Richard Goode, Mary Stewart Hammond, Kate Handley, Beth Harrison, Heidi Hart, Helen Hecht, Bill Henderson, Edward Hirsch, John Hollander, Bill Holm, Cheryl Hurley, Galway Kinnell, Susan Kinsolving, Patricia Leonard, Virginia Mailman, Lisel Museller, John Naughton, Ramon Ortega-Cowan, Nils Peterson, Robert

Phillips, Constance Pratt, Grace Schulman, Harvey Shapiro, William Jay Smith, Tree Swenson, Ann Thorne, Margo Viscusi, and William Warren.

We are especially grateful to our publishers, Karen Braziller and Michael Braziller, who have devoted very valuable and thoughtful attention to our work; to Gabe Fried, Persea's gifted poetry editor and poet, for believing in the book, for his guidance and suggestions, and for his tact and trust in our judgment: we cannot imagine the book without him; to Lytton Smith, Rita Lascaro, and Enid Stubin; to Jeannette Watson Sanger and Ione Strum for their enthusiastic and invaluable responses from the beginning; to Kenneth Fields, inspired teacher and poet for his great contributions; to Carol Muske-Dukes, who read portions of the manuscript in its early stages and whose lively mind and support are extraordinary; to Bill Handley, for his wide-ranging imagination and knowledge of both poetry and music, for his wit, *joie de vivre*, and responsiveness; and to J. D. McClatchy, for his exceptional generosity with his dazzling talents as poet, librettist, critic, teacher, and editor—gifts that have enriched American arts and letters.

Our first and last thanks are to our husbands, Frank Houghton and Paul Draper, for their interest and delight in our discoveries—and for listening with us, *ensemble*.

Helen Handley Houghton
New York City

Maureen McCarthy Draper
Cupertino, California

August 2007

Listening to Music

Czeslaw Milosz

In Music

Wailing of a flute, a little drum.
A small wedding cortège accompanies a couple
Going past clay houses in the street of a village.
In the dress of the bride much white satin.
How many renunciations to sew it, once in a lifetime.
The dress of the groom black, festively stiff.
The flute tells something of the hills, parched, the color of deer.
Hens scratch in dry mounds of manure.

I have not seen it, I summoned it listening to music.
The instruments play for themselves, in their own eternity.
Lips blow, agile fingers work, so short a time.
Soon afterward the pageant sinks into the earth.
But the sound endures, autonomous, triumphant,
Forever visited by, each time returning,
The warm touch of cheeks, interiors of houses,
And particular human lives
Of which the chronicles make no mention.

(Translated by the author and Robert Hass)

Edna St. Vincent Millay

On Hearing a Symphony of Beethoven

Sweet sounds, oh, beautiful music, do not cease!
Reject me not into the world again.
With you alone is excellence and peace,
Mankind made plausible, his purpose plain.
Enchanted in your air benign and shrewd,
With limbs a-sprawl and empty faces pale,
The spiteful and the stingy and the rude
Sleep like the scullions in the fairy-tale.
This moment is the best the world can give:
The tranquil blossom on the tortured stem.
Reject me not, sweet sounds! oh, let me live,
Till Doom espy my towers and scatter them,
A city spell-bound under the aging sun,
Music my rampart, and my only one.

Bill Holm

from MAGNIFICAT

The music begins. It curls, laves
exalts, weeps, thumps, celebrates.
Every two minutes a new galaxy
dances through damp church air
into the ears, then the body—
ribbons of stars, garlands of planets,
space full of nothing but light.
It unlocks me and I weep . . .

Dick Davis

LISTENING

Sweet Reason rules the morning—what's as sweet as
Rosalyn Tureck playing Bach partitas?

Midday's for Haydn, who loved everyone
(Except that pompous pig Napoleon)—
Music's Hippocrates ("First do no harm"),
An *Aufklärung* of common sense and charm.

Mozart and Schubert own the afternoon—
High spirits and a Fiordiligi swoon;
A sudden key change: you will die alone.
The shadow that you stare at is your own.

Then comes the night. Pandora's lid is lifted,
Each scene implodes before it can be shifted—
Longing's a tenor's accurate bravura,
Sex and Despair are *Fach* and *Tessitura:*

And heaven's where the mind's sopranos sing
In harmonies undreamt of in *The Ring.*

Robert Bly

LISTENING TO THE KÖLN CONCERT

After we had loved each other intently,
we heard notes tumbling together,
in late winter, and we heard ice
falling from the ends of twigs.

The notes abandon so much as they move.
They are the food not eaten, the comfort
not taken, the lies not spoken.
The music is my attention to you.

And when the music came again,
later in the day, I saw tears in your eyes.
I saw you turn your face away
so that the others would not see.

When men and women come together,
how much they have to abandon! Wrens
make their nests of fancy threads
and string ends, animals

abandon all their money each year.
What is it that men and women leave?
Harder than wrens' doing, they have
to abandon their longing for the perfect.

The inner nest not made by instinct
will never be quite round,
and each has to enter the nest
made by the other imperfect bird.

B. H. Fairchild

The Dumka

His parents would sit alone together
on the blue divan in the small living room
listening to Dvorak's piano quintet.
They would sit there in their old age,
side by side, quite still, backs rigid, hands
in their laps, and look straight ahead
at the yellow light of the phonograph
that seemed as distant as a lamplit
window seen across the plains late at night.
They would sit quietly as something dense

and radiant swirled around them, something
like the dust storms of the thirties that began
smearing the sky green with doom
but afterwards drenched the air with an amber
glow and then vanished, leaving profiles
of children on pillows and a pale gauze
over mantles and table tops. But it was
the memory of dust that encircled them now
and made them smile faintly and raise
or bow their heads as they spoke about

the farm in twilight with piano music
spiraling out across red roads and fields
of maize, bread lines in the city, women
and men lining main street like mannequins,
and then the war, the white frame rent house,
and the homecoming, the homecoming,
the homecoming, and afterwards, green lawns

and a new piano with its mahogany gleam
like pond ice at dawn, and now alone
in the house in the vanishing neighborhood,

the slow mornings of coffee and newspapers
and evenings of music and scattered bits
of talk like leaves suddenly fallen before
one notices the new season. And they would sit
there alone and soon he would reach across
and lift her hand as if it were the last unbroken
leaf and he would hold her hand in his hand
for a long time and they would look far off
into the music of their lives as they sat alone
together in the room in the house in Kansas.

Eavan Boland

FOND MEMORY

It was a school where all the children wore darned worsted,
where they cried—or almost all—when the Reverend Mother
announced at lunchtime that the King had died

peacefully in his sleep. I dressed in wool as well,
ate rationed food, played English games and learned
how wise the Magna Carta was, how hard the Hanoverians

had tried, the measure and complexity of verse,
the hum and score of the whole orchestra.
At three o'clock I caught two buses home

where sometimes in the late afternoon
at a piano pushed into the corner of the playroom
my father would sit down and play the slow

lilts of Tom Moore while I stood there trying
not to weep at the cigarette smoke stinging up
from his fingers and—as much as I could think—

I thought this is my country, was, will be again,
this upward-straining song made to be
our safe inventory of pain. And I was wrong.

Issa

Blossoms at night
and the faces of people
moved by music.

(Translated by Robert Hass)

Edward Hirsch

SONATA

For Janet

Wake up and listen, tonight
the dark wind trembles in the pines
like the nervous hands of a young girl

playing a sonata for her grandmother
for the first time, or like
the spindly legs of an old woman

walking home through a field of stumped
elms buried in the fog. The girl
hits the wrong note, just once, and

suddenly the old woman begins to hum,
loudly and out of tune, a cradle song
to ward off the darkest shadows.

Wake up! And wake my mother
in her bed and your mother in her bed,
my grandmother in her coffin. Wake up

our daughters and granddaughters still unborn.
Tonight the wind is playing the same song
over and over again, the same sonata,

yes, with the same wrong note
relentless as time, unbearable and human

Linda Pastan

MUSE

No angel speaks to me.
And though the wind
plucks the dry leaves
as if they were so many notes
of music, I can hear no words.

Still, I listen. I search
the feathery shapes of clouds
hoping to find the curve of a wing.
And sometimes, when the static
of the world clears just for a moment

a small voice comes through,
chastening. Music
is its own language, it says.
Along the indifferent corridors
of space, angels could be hiding.

Michael Ryan

EARPHONES

Autumn in our kitchen, hooked up
to a discman (Bach's Sonatas and Partitas for Solo Violin),
I become the music with earphones on:
no noise-as-usual inside my skull,
I can do things so the doing seems to be coming
from not-me, I am so expert and prolific
at rutabaga soup, peeling and chopping with such prowess,
spicing with panache, fussily tasting and adjusting,
even cleaning the pot and utensils, wiping the counter,
the sink, the cutting board—so happy, my darling,
that I despite myself have made something good for you
you will never have to suffer or work for.
Look, it's waiting in your favorite blue bowl
with fresh bread and wine beside it.
Come, sit, my loveliness, my blessing:
Come, sit, and eat it with me.

Henry Taylor

Elevator Music

A tune with no more substance than the air,
performed on underwater instruments,
is proper to this short lift from the earth.
It hovers as we draw into ourselves
and turn our reverent eyes toward the lights
that count us to our various destinies.
We're all in this together, the song says,
and later we'll descend. The melody
is like a name we don't recall just now
that still keeps on insisting it is there.

Stephen Dobyns

LOUD MUSIC

My stepdaughter and I circle round and round.
You see, I like the music loud, the speakers
throbbing, jam-packing the room with sound whether
Bach or rock and roll, the volume cranked up so
each bass note is like a hand smacking the gut.
But my stepdaughter disagrees. She is four
and likes the music decorous, pitched below
her own voice—that tenuous projection of self.
With music blasting, she feels she disappears,
is lost within the blare, which in fact I like.
But at four what she wants is self-location
and uses her voice as a porpoise uses
its sonar: to find herself in all this space.
If she had a sort of box with a peephole
and looked inside, what she'd like to see would be
herself standing there in her red pants, jacket,
yellow plastic lunch box: a proper subject
for serious study. But me, if I raised
the same box to my eye, I would wish to find
the ocean on one of those days when wind
and thick cloud make the water gray and restless
as if some creature brooded underneath,
a rocky coast with a road along the shore
where someone like me was walking and has gone.

Billy Collins

Sunday Morning with the Sensational Nightingales

It was not the Five Mississippi Blind Boys
who lifted me off the ground
that Sunday morning
as I drove down for the paper, some oranges, and bread.
Nor was it the Dixie Hummingbirds
or the Soul Stirrers, despite their quickening name,
or even the Swan Silvertones
who inspired me to look over the commotion of trees
into the open vault of the sky.

No, it was the Sensational Nightingales
who happened to be singing on the gospel
station early that Sunday morning
and must be credited with the bumping up
of my spirit, the arousal of the mice within.

I have always loved this harmony,
like four, sometimes five trains running
side by side over a contoured landscape—
make that a shimmering, red-dirt landscape,
wildflowers growing along the silver tracks,
lace tablecloths covering the hills,
the men and women in white shirts and dresses
walking in the direction of a tall steeple.
Sunday morning in a perfect Georgia.
But I am not here to describe the sound
of the falsetto whine, sepulchral bass,
alto and tenor fitted snugly in between;

Only to witness my own minor ascension
that morning as they sang, so parallel,
about the usual themes,
the garden of suffering,
the beads of blood on the forehead,
the stone before the hillside tomb,
and the ancient rolling waters
we would all have to cross some day.

God bless the Sensational Nightingales,
I thought as I turned up the volume,
God bless their families and their powder blue suits.
They are a far cry from the quiet kneeling
I was raised with,
a far, hand-clapping cry from the candles
that glowed in the alcoves
and the fixed eyes of saints staring down
from their corners.

Oh, my cap was on straight that Sunday morning
and I was fine keeping the car on the road.
No one would ever have guessed
I was being lifted into the air by nightingales,
hoisted by their beaks like a long banner
that curls across an empty blue sky,
caught up in the annunciation
of these high, most encouraging tidings.

Cornelius Eady

RADIO

There is the woman
Who will not listen
To music. There is the man
Who dreams of kissing the lips
Attached to the voice.
There is the singer
Who reinvents the world
In musical notation.
There is the young couple
Who dance slowly on the sidewalk,
As if the rest of the street
Didn't exist.
There is the school boy
Whose one possession
Is an electric box
That scrambles the neighborhood.
There is the young girl
Who locks her bedroom door,
And lip-syncs in the mirror.
There is the young beau
Who believes in the songs so much,
He hears them
Even when
He isn't kissing someone.
There is the mother
Who absent-mindedly sways to the beat
But fears the implications
For her daughter.

There is the man
Who carries one in his
Breast pocket
And pretends it's a Luger.
There are the two young punks
Who lug one into our car
On the stalled D train,
Who, as we tense for the assault,
Tune in a classical music station,
As if this were
Saturday night
On another world.

Daniel Hall

COUNTRY RADIO

It will be late (maybe too late, this worry
        keeping you from falling back to sleep)
when from around the corner or up the alley some
        convergence of bright voices
will rise to your window, cries of, what, fear
        or laughter, nothing coming clear to you

in your bed, the heart of winter, the refrigerator
        shuddering on or off.
Or they will have crested already by the time you've
        come to completely, the flow
stalled, turning outward, out from the muffle of
        bedding, the cold room, away from you,

further and further. And in their wake you'll tune
        in a signal, clearer and clearer:
midsummer, long past midnight, how the milk train
        would come dragging its dim racket out
between the farms, the passengers slumped and gently
        rocking, one man still wide-awake,

spark-lit, gazing ahead into the humid dark, a
        cool brilliance spilling over
the dry fields and cinders of the only world you
        knew. "From New York," your forbidden
transistor whispered, the audience rustling like
        grass between breezes . . . And the baton

will rise over a piece that refuses to play itself
        out as written, reworked
some nights to the point of madness, fragments
        lunging and leapfrogging in their frenzy
for resolution— Then listen, listen to me, and
        you'll hear the entire passage.

Lisel Mueller

THE POWER OF MUSIC TO DISTURB

A humid night. Mad June bugs dash themselves
against a window they should know is there;
I hear an owl awaking in the woods
behind our house, and wonder if it shakes
sleep from its eyes and lets its talons play,
stretch and retract, rehearsing for the kill—
and on the radio the music drives
toward death by love, for love, because of love
like some black wave that cannot break itself.

It is a music that luxuriates
in the impossibilities ot love
and rides frustration till two ghosts become
alive again, aware of how the end
of every act of love is separateness;
raw, ruthless lovers, desperate enough
to bank on the absurdity of death
for royal consummation, permanence
of feeling, having, knowing, holding on.

My God, he was a devil of a man
who wrote this music so voluptuous
it sucks me in with possibilities
of sense and soul, of pity and desire
which place and time make ludicrous: I sit
across from you here in our living room
with chairs and books and red geraniums
and ordinary lamplight on the floor
after an ordinary day of love.

How can disaster be so beautiful?
I range the beaches of our lucid world
against that flood, trying to think about
our child upstairs, asleep with her light on
to keep her from vague evils; about us
whose loving has become so natural
that it has rid itself of teeth and claws,
implements for the lovers new at love,
whose jitters goad them into drawing blood.

But O my love, I cannot beat it back,
neither the sound nor what the sound lets loose;
the opulence of agony drowns out
the hard, dry smack of death against the glass
and batters down the seawalls of my mind,
and I am pulled to levels below light
where easy ways of love are meaningless
and creatures feel their way along the dark
by shock of ecstasy and heat of pain.

Charles Baudelaire

MUSIC

Music often takes me like a sea
      and I set out
under mist or a transparent sky
      for my pale star;

I run before the wind as if I had
      laid on full sail,
climbing the mountainous backs of the waves,
      plummeting down

in darkness, eardrums throbbing as I feel
      the coming wreck;
fair winds or foul—a raging storm

      on the great deep
my cradle, and dead calm the looking-glass
      of my despair!

(Translated by Richard Howard)

Li Yi

ON HEARING A FLUTE AT NIGHT
FROM THE WALL OF SHOU-HSIANG

The sand below the border-mountain lies like snow,
And the moon like frost beyond the city wall,
And someone somewhere, playing a flute,
Has made the soldiers homesick all night long.

(Translated by Witter Bynner)

Liam Rector

THE EVENTUAL MUSIC

For David St. John

Eventually someone knocks at your door eventually
just as the moon is eventual and just
as you were thinking that the only trust
is the trust of meat, the shift of need
and eventually someone knocks and you stand
at your own door   and you know then
that you are the door-opener and that someone
will enter, and someone does   and you tell someone
that you have been holding the world in its place,
in its place without music   you tell her
that fashion goes deep, fear goes deeper,
that you are intrigued by the chemistry
of what comes next   and someone eventually announces
that she is actually here and has arrived with music boxes,
tiny porcelain objects that never leave,
always stay and always music   she apologizes
for having come so late to your door   and you speak to her
of the bones that deny the music, of the arteries
and their race towards the skin, of the blood
that hears music always and eventually
runs away from home

and you lie down, with someone, in your opened door
and you hear all that music that was not there before.

Emily Dickinson

Heart, not so heavy as mine
Wending late home—
As it passed my window
Whistled itself a tune—
A careless snatch—a ballad—
A ditty of the street—
Yet to my irritated Ear
An Anodyne so sweet—
It was as if a Bobolink
Sauntering this way
Carolled, and paused, and carolled—
Then bubbled slow away!
It was as if a chirping brook
Upon a dusty way—
Set bleeding feet to minuets
Without the knowing why!
Tomorrow, night will come again—
Perhaps, weary and sore—
Ah Bugle! By my window
I pray you pass once more.

Robert Herrick

To Music, to Becalm His Fever

Charm me asleep, and melt me so
    With thy delicious numbers;
That being ravished, hence I go
    Away in easy slumbers.
        Ease my sick head,
        And make my bed,
Thou Power that canst sever
        From me this ill:
        And quickly still:
        Though thou not kill
           My fever.

Thou sweetly canst convert the same
    From a consuming fire,
Into a gentle-licking flame,
    And make it thus expire.
        Then make me weep
        My pains asleep;
And give me such reposes,
        That I, poor I,
        May think, thereby,
        I live and die
           'Mongst roses.

Fall on me like a silent dew,
    Or like those maiden showers,
Which, by the peep of day, do strew
    A baptime o'er the flowers.
        Melt, melt my pains,
        With thy soft strains;

That having ease me given,
With full delight,
I leave this light;
And take my flight
For Heaven.

May Sarton

EVENING MUSIC

We enter this evening as we enter a quartet
Listening again for its particular note
The interval where all seems possible,
Order within time when action is suspended
And we are pure in heart, perfect in will.
We enter the evening whole and well-defended
But at the quick of self, intense detachment
That is a point of burning far from passion—
And this, we know, is what we always meant
And even love must learn it in some fashion,
To move like formal music through the heart,
To be achieved like some high difficult art.

We enter the evening as we enter a quartet
Listening again for its particular note
Which is your note, perhaps, your special gift,
A detached joy that flowers and makes bloom
The longest silence in the silent room—
And there would be no music if you left.

James Merrill

THE VICTOR DOG

For Elizabeth Bishop

Bix to Buxtehude to Boulez,
The little white dog on the Victor label
Listens long and hard as he is able.
It's all in a day's work, whatever plays.

From judgment, it would seem, he has refrained.
He even listens earnestly to Bloch,
Then builds a church upon our acid rock.
He's man's—no—he's the Leiermann's best friend,

Or would be if hearing and listening were the same.
Does he hear? I fancy he rather smells
Those lemon-gold arpeggios in Ravel's
"Les jets d'eau du palais de ceux qui s'aiment."

He ponders the Schumann Concerto's tall willow hit
By lightning, and stays put. When he surmises
Through one of Bach's eternal boxwood mazes
The oboe pungent as a bitch in heat,

Or when the calypso decants its raw bay rum
Or the moon in *Wozzeck* reddens ripe for murder,
He doesn't sneeze or howl; just listens harder.
Adamant needles bear down on him from

Whirling of outer space, too black, too near—
But he was taught as a puppy not to flinch,
Mush less to imitate his bête noire Blanche
Who barked, fat foolish creature, at King Lear.

Still others fought in the road's filth over Jezebel,
Slavered on hearths of horned and pelted barons.
His forebears lacked, to say the least, forbearance.
Can nature change in him? Nothing's impossible.

The last chord fades. The night is cold and fine.
His master's voice rasps through the grooves' bare groves.
Obediently, in silence like the grave's
He sleeps there on the still-warm gramophone

Only to dream he is at the première of a Handel
Opera long thought lost—*Il Cane Minore.*
Its allegorical subject is his story!
A little dog revolving round a spindle

Gives rise to harmonies beyond belief,
A cast of stars . . . Is there in Victor's heart
No honey for the vanquished? Art is art.
The life it asks of us is a dog's life.

Henri Coulette

A ONE-EYED CAT NAMED HATHAWAY

A one-eyed cat named Hathaway on my lap,
A fire in the fireplace, and Schubert's 5th
All silvery somewhere on a radio
I barely hear, but hear—this is, I think,
As close as I may come to happiness.

Songs & Singing

Galway Kinnell

THE CHOIR

Little beings with their hair blooming
so differently on skulls of odd sizes
and their eyes serious and their jaws
very firm from singing in Gilead, and with
their mouths gaping, saying
"Ah!" for God,
"O!" for an alphabet of O's,
they stand in rows, each suspended
from a fishing line
hooked at the breastbone, being hauled up
toward the heavenly gases.

Everyone who truly sings is beautiful.
Even sad music
requires an absolute happiness:
eyes, nostrils, mouth strain together in quintal harmony
to sing Joy and Death well.

Anne Porter

MUSIC

When I was a child
I once sat sobbing on the floor
Beside my mother's piano
As she played and sang
For there was in her singing
A shy yet solemn glory
My smallness could not hold

And when I was asked
Why I was crying
I had no words for it
I only shook my head
And went on crying

Why is it that music
At its most beautiful
Opens a wound in us
An ache a desolation
Deep as a homesickness
For some far-off
And half-forgotten country

I've never understood
Why this is so

But there's an ancient legend
From the other side of the world
That gives away the secret
Of this mysterious sorrow
For centuries on centuries

We have been wandering
But we were made for Paradise
As deer for the forest

And when music comes to us
With its heavenly beauty
It brings us desolation
For when we hear it
We half remember
That lost native country

We dimly remember the fields
Their fragrant windswept clover
The birdsongs in the orchards
The wild white violets in the moss
By the transparent streams

And shining at the heart of it
Is the longed-for beauty
Of the One who waits for us
Who will always wait for us
In those radiant meadows

Yet also came to live with us
And wanders where we wander.

Li-Young Lee

I ASK MY MOTHER TO SING

She begins, and my grandmother joins her.
Mother and daughter sing like young girls.
If my father were alive, he would play
his accordion and sway like a boat.

I've never been in Peking, or the Summer Palace,
nor stood on the great Stone Boat to watch
the rain begin on Kuen Ming Lake, the picnickers
running away in the grass.

But I love to hear it sung;
how the waterlilies fill with rain until
they overturn, spilling water into water,
then rock back, and fill with more.

Both women have begun to cry.
But neither stops her song.

Adam Zagajewski

WHERE THE BREATH IS

She stands alone onstage
and has no instrument.

She lays her palms upon her breast,
where the breath is born
and where it dies.

The palms do not sing,
nor does the breast.

What sings is what stays silent.

Philip Levine

SONGS

Dawn coming in over the fields
of darkness takes me by surprise
and I look up from my solitary road
pleased not to be alone, the birds
now choiring from the orange groves
huddling to the low hills. But sorry
that this night has ended, a night
in which you spoke of how little love
we seemed to have known and all of it
going from one of us to the other.
You could tell the words took me
by surprise, as they often will, and you
grew shy and held me away for a while,
your eyes enormous in the darkness,
almost as large as your hunger
to see and be seen over and over.

30 years ago I heard a woman sing
of the motherless child sometimes
she felt like. In a white dress
this black woman with a gardenia
in her hair leaned on the piano
and stared out into the breathing darkness
of unknown men and women needing
her songs. There were those among
us who cried, those who rejoiced
that she was back before us for a time,
a time not to be much longer, for
the voice was going and the habits
slowly becoming all there was of her.

And I believe that night she cared
for the purity of the songs and not
much else. Oh, she still saw
the slow gathering of that red dusk
that hovered over her cities, and no
doubt dawns like this one caught
her on the roads from job to job
but the words she'd lived by were
drained of mystery as this sky
is now, and there was no more "Easy
Living" and she was "Miss Brown" to
no one and no one was her "Lover Man."
The only songs that mattered were wordless
like those rising in confusion from
the trees or wind-songs that waken
the grass that slept a century, that
waken me to how far we've come.

Mark Doty

from MESSIAH (CHRISTMAS PORTION)

     Aren't we enlarged
by the scale of what we're able
to desire? Everything,
     the choir insists,

     might flame;
inside these wrappings
burns another, brighter life,
     quickened, now,

     by song: hear how
it cascades, in overlapping,
lapidary waves of praise? Still time.
     Still time to change.

Lisel Mueller

JOY

Don't cry, it's only music,
someone's voice is saying;
no one you love is dying.

It's only music. And it was only spring,
the world's unreasoning body
run amok, like a saint's, with glory,
that overwhelmed a young girl
into unreasoning sadness.
Crazy, she told herself,
I should be dancing with happiness.

But it happened again. It happens
when we make bottomless love—
there follows a bottomless sadness
which is not despair
but its nameless opposite.
It has nothing to do with the passing of time.
It's not about loss. It's about
two seemingly parallel lines
suddenly coming together
inside us, in some place
that is still wilderness.

Joy, joy, the sopranos sing,
reaching for the shimmering notes
while our eyes fill with tears.

Seamus Heaney

THE SINGER'S HOUSE

When they said *Carrickfergus* I could hear
the frosty echo of saltminers' picks.
I imagined it, chambered and glinting,
a township built of light.

What do we say any more
to conjure the salt of our earth?
So much comes and is gone
that should be crystal and kept,

and amicable weathers
that bring up the grain of things,
their tang of season and store,
are all the packing we'll get.

So I say to myself *Gweebarra*
and its music hits off the place
like water hitting off granite.
I see the glittering sound

framed in your window,
knives and forks set on oilcloth,
and the seals' heads, suddenly outlined,
scanning everything.

People here used to believe
that drowned souls lived in the seals.
At spring tides they might change shape.
They loved music and swam in for a singer

who might stand at the end of summer
in the mouth of a whitewashed turf-shed,
his shoulder to the jamb, his song
a rowboat far out in evening.

When I came here first you were always singing,
a hint of the clip of the pick
in your winnowing climb and attack.
Raise it again, man. We still believe what we hear.

Galway Kinnell

FIRST SONG

Then it was dusk in Illinois, the small boy
After an afternoon of carting dung
Hung on the rail fence, a sapped thing
Weary to crying. Dark was growing tall
And he began to hear the pond frogs all
Calling on his ear with what seemed their joy.

Soon their sound was pleasant for a boy
Listening in the smoky dusk and the nightfall
Of Illinois, and from the fields two small
Boys came bearing cornstalk violins
And they rubbed the cornstalk bows with resins
And the three sat there scraping of their joy.

It was now fine music the frogs and the boys
Did in the towering Illinois twilight make
And into dark in spite of a shoulder's ache
A boy's hunched body loved out of a stalk
The first song of his happiness, and the song woke
His heart to the darkness and into the sadness of joy.

Emily Dickinson

I shall keep singing!
Birds will pass me
On their way to Yellower Climes—
Each—with a Robin's expectation—
I—with my Redbreast—
And my Rhymes—

Late—when I take my place in summer—
But—I shall bring a fuller tune—
Vespers—are sweeter than Matins—Signor—
Morning—only the seed of Noon—

Siegfried Sassoon

Everyone Sang

Everyone suddenly burst out singing;
And I was filled with such delight
As prisoned birds must find in freedom,
Winging wildly across the white
Orchards and dark-green fields; on—on—and out of sight.

Everyone's voice was suddenly lifted;
And beauty came like the setting sun:
My heart was shaken with tears; and horror
Drifted away...O, but Everyone
Was a bird; and the song was wordless; the singing will never
    be done.

W. H. Auden

THE COMPOSER

All the others translate: the painter sketches
A visible world to love or reject;
Rummaging into his living, the poet fetches
The images out that hurt and connect.

From Life to Art by painstaking adaption,
Relying on us to cover the rift;
Only your notes are pure contraption,
Only your song is an absolute gift.

Pour out your presence, O delight, cascading
The falls of the knee and the weirs of the spine,
Our climate of silence and doubt invading;

You alone, alone, O imaginary song,
Are unable to say an existence is wrong,
And pour out your forgiveness like a wine.

Thomas Lux

REGARDING (MOST) SONGS

Whatever is too stupid to say can be sung.
        —Joseph Addison (1672–1719)

The human voice can sing a vowel to break your heart.
It trills a string of banal words,
but your blood jumps, regardless. You don't care
about the words but only *how* they're sung
and the music behind—the brass, the drums.
Oh the primal, necessary drums
behind the words so dumb!
That power, the bang and the boom and again the bang
we cannot, need not, live without,
nor without other means to make sweet noise,
the guitar or violin, the things that sing
the plaintive, joyful sounds.
Which is why I like songs best
when I can't hear the words, or, better still,
when there are no words at all.

Elizabeth Bishop

SONNET

I am in need of music that would flow
Over my fretful, feeling finger-tips,
Over my bitter-tainted, trembling lips,
With melody, deep, clear, and liquid-slow.
Oh, for the healing swaying, old and low,
Of some song sung to rest the tired dead,
A song to fall like water on my head,
And over quivering limbs, dream flushed to glow!

There is a magic made by melody:
A spell of rest, and quiet breath, and cool
Heart, that sinks through fading colors deep
To the subaqueous stillness of the sea,
And floats forever in a moon-green pool,
Held in the arms of rhythm and of sleep.

Dorianne Laux

SINGING BACK THE WORLD

I don't remember how it began.
The singing. Judy at the wheel
in the middle of *Sentimental Journey*.
The side of her face glowing.
Her full lips moving. Beyond her shoulder
the little houses sliding by.
And Geri. Her frizzy hair tumbling
in the wind wing's breeze, fumbling
with the words. All of us singing
as loud as we can. Off key.
Not even a semblance of harmony.
Driving home in a blue Comet singing
I'll be Seeing You and *Love Is a Rose*.
The love songs of war. The war songs
of love. Mixing up verses, eras, words.
Songs from stupid musicals.
Coming in strong on the easy refrains.
Straining our middle aged voices
trying to reach impossible notes,
reconstruct forgotten phrases.
Cole Porter's *Anything Goes*.
Shamelessly la la la-ing
whole sections. Forgetting
the rent, the kids, the men,
the other woman. The sad goodbye.
The whole of childhood. Forgetting
the lost dog. Polio. The grey planes
pregnant with bombs. Fields
of white headstones. All of it gone
as we struggle to remember

the words. One of us picking up
where the others leave off. Intent
on the song. Forgetting our bodies,
their pitiful limbs, their heaviness.
Nothing but three throats
beating back the world—Laurie's
radiation treatments. The scars
on Christina's arms. Kim's brother.
Molly's grandfather. Jane's sister.
Singing to the telephone poles
skimming by. Stoplights
blooming green. The road,
a glassy black river edged
with brilliant gilded weeds. The car
an immense boat cutting the air
into blue angelic plumes. Singing
Blue Moon and *Paper Moon*
and *Mack the Knife*, and *Nobody Knows*
the Trouble I've Seen.

Jill Bialosky

Music Lesson

I thought I was like her.
I would have sung, played the violin, piano, flute,
made music my life's work. I could hear the rapture;
the sound of the metronome as we stood straight,
chin up, heels of our Mary Janes
and loafers against the wood step.
Sometimes on the way to school,
I felt a melody build in the cave
of my body like a sudden
brightness just before letting go.
In assembly we stood in tiers depending
on our height as if we were the chorus
on the steps of the Theatre of Dionysus
looking into the hollow stage
in anticipation of a great tragedy.
We followed the tempo
against the movement of our maestro's stick,
watched the O of her lips
as she mouthed the words. I concentrated.
I let the air fill my diaphragm
just as she instructed.
Once I looked away from her
and turned, just a quick glimpse, to look at him.
Like Narcissus, he would have found a pool,
a lake, his image in the glass of the music room's window
and looked at his reflection all day. Still,
like a love-struck nymph (I was only a child)
I liked to watch.
To feel the light brush of his breath
on the back of my neck as he sang.

My country 'tis of thee
sweet land of liberty
of thee I sing;
land where our fathers died . . .
I sang louder, inhaling the air
and allowing it to sail through my being
until it was no longer me but the notes
of a beautiful bird dispatched
of her doom to echo the same notes
who had at last found her voice.
But it was too late.
In that one glance of betrayal
she saw inside the hidden chamber
my true self inhabited
and deemed to silence it.
My teacher looked at me
and put her index finger over her stern lips.
I never sang again. I was quiet.

Susan Kinsolving

HALF NOTE

Next to each other, it's secrets we want
to share, closing the distance between bed

and chair, dark as the path turning our steps
in the night, deep as Scarlatti played

without light. When the body begins its
counterpoint to the brain, rhythms grow harder

and harder to train. For days, I withheld
one hand from you. But one-handed, your music

played through, touching me, as if by two.

Peter Schmitt

TIN EAR

We stood at attention as she moved
with a kind of Groucho shuffle
down our line, her trained music
teacher's ear passing by
our ten- and eleven-year-old mouths
open to some song now forgotten.
And as she held her momentary
pause in front of me, I peered
from the corner of my eye
to hers, and knew the truth
I had suspected.
In the following days,
as certain of our peers
disappeared at appointed hours
for the Chorus, something in me
was already closing shop.
Indeed, to this day
I still clam up
for the national anthem
in crowded stadiums, draw
disapproving alumni stares
as I smile the length of school songs,
and even hum and clap
through "Happy Birthday," creating
a diversion—all lest I send
the collective pitch
careening headlong into dissonance.
It's only in the choice acoustics
of shower and sealed car
that I can finally give voice

to that heart deep within me
that is pure, tonally perfect, music.
But when the water stops running
and the radio's off, I can remember
that day in class,
when I knew for the first time
that mine would be a world of words
without melody, where *refrain*
means *do not join,*
where I'm ready to sing
in a key no one has ever heard.

David Huddle

Ooly Pop a Cow

For Bess and Molly

My brother Charles
brought home the news
the kids were saying
take a flying leap
and eat me raw
and be bop a lula.

Forty miles he rode
the bus there and back.
The dog and I met him
at the door, panting
for hoke poke, hoke
de waddy waddy hoke poke.

In Cu Chi, Vietnam,
I heard tapes somebody's
sister sent of wild thing,
I think I love you
and hey now, what's that
sound, everybody look what's . . .

Now it's my daughters
bringing home no-duh
rock-out, whatever,
like I totally
paused, and like
I'm like . . .

I'm like Mother, her hands
in biscuit dough,
her ears turning red
from ain' nothin butta,
blue monday, and
tutti frutti, aw rooty!

Tony Hoagland

YOU'RE THE TOP

Of all the people that I've ever known
I think my grandmother Bernice
would be best qualified to be beside me now

driving north of Boston in a rented car
while Cole Porter warbles on the radio;
only she would be trivial and un-

politically correct enough to totally enjoy
the rhyming of *Mahatma Gandhi*
with *Napoleon brandy*;

and she would understand, from 1948,
the miracle that once was cellophane,
which Porter rhymes with *night in Spain*.

She loved that image of the high gay life
where people dressed by servants
turned every night into the Ritz:

dancing through a shower of just
uncorked champagne
into the shelter of a dry martini.

When she was 70 and I was young
I hated how a life of privilege
had kept her ignorance intact

about the world beneath her pretty feet,
how she believed that people with good manners
naturally had yachts, knew how to waltz

and dribbled French into their sentences
like salad dressing. My liberal adolescent rage
was like a righteous fist back then

that wouldn't let me rest,
but I've come far enough from who I was
to see her as she saw herself:

a tipsy debutante in 1938,
kicking off a party with her shoes;
launching the lipstick-red high heel from her elegant big toe

into the orbit of a chandelier
suspended in a lyric by Cole Porter,
bright and beautiful and useless.

Bill Holm

BLIZZARD

After midnight the blizzard howls itself out,
the wind sleeps, a tired lover.
Before bed, I think of you
and play the *Meistersinger* quintet
over and over, singing
along on all the parts,
dancing through the house
like a polar bear who thinks
it has joined the ballet.
You are in my arms, dancing too;
whirling from room to room;
frost crusted on the window
begins to glow like lit up faces.
My five fingers, now on fire
like these five voices singing,
imagine touching the skin
over your shoulders.

Carol Muske-Dukes

THE ROSE: 1984

Annie, it was the first full moon after equinox—and we drove
after dinner with you asleep, to the new house where you will
grow up. As we drove, your father and I sang along with a
popular song on the radio, a sad thoughtful ballad about dying
and being born again. A friend of his had written it and he
described how she got it, word by word, then sang it piecemeal
to her friends. Now it's just famous and people sing it without
thinking, as we do when we know things by heart. For my part,
I knew how he felt telling the story, thinking of the forming
lyric, the steady resistance of the accelerator pedal under his
foot, the cool wind ruffling up one side of his hair as he drove,
as he remembered aloud. I suppose he felt me worrying without
thinking, as I do, my foot against the floor on my side, braking
out of habit.

We kept looking back at you in the car seat, your head rolled
back in its sun hat, striped by the full moon, your dreams your
own as you slept. Amanda's song on the radio, our voices joined
then diverging into harmony and your steady breathing into a
starry background you would inhabit only briefly, already bored
with the fame of babies. The moon rising into the gold of its
billionth pressing, the new moon inside it already an embryo—
your infant dreams follow each other one by one, till they're all
a single thing—like the melody still carrying us when memory
suspends a word here and there. I try to remember how I felt
carrying you, but I can only imagine it, a kind of fame—part
of the well-known Ongoing, each little physical dream forgotten.
But this—the moon rising, The Rose on our lips—completely
sentimental the carrying of the tune—Annie, his hand on the
wheel, the way he sang.

Gregory Orr

His song was about the world,
She sang of what she saw,
And yet it was always
The beloved's own being
That was the theme
Of that beautiful music.

Sometimes it was words,
Sometimes only the body's
Movements or an expression
Fleeting across the face.

And now the singer himself
Has fled. Now her silence
Is absolute.

Now I open the Book
Hoping to hear that song again.

Sappho

from THE WEDDING OF EKTOR
AND ANDROMAKHA

A long parade sings its way from the sea.
The flutes are keen and the drums tight;
Charmed air holds the young girls' songs.
Along the way the people bring them bowls
Of cassia, cups of olibanum and myrrh.
Dancing grandmothers shout the marriage song.
Men and boys march and sing to Páon,
To Apollo of the harp, archer of archers,
And sing that Ektor and Andrómakha
Are like two of the gods together.

(Translated by Guy Davenport)

Rumi

WHERE EVERYTHING IS MUSIC

Don't worry about saving these songs!
And if one of our instruments breaks,
it doesn't matter.

We have fallen into the place
where everything is music.

The strumming and the flute notes
rise into the atmosphere,
And even if the whole world's harp
should burn up, there will still be
hidden instruments playing.

So the candle flickers and goes out.
We have a piece of flint, and a spark.

This singing art is sea foam.
The graceful movements come from a pearl
somewhere on the ocean floor.

Poems reach up like spindrift and the edge
of driftwood along the beach, wanting!

They derive
from a slow and powerful root
that we can't see.

Stop the words now.
Open the window in the center of your chest,
and let the spirits fly in and out.

(Translated by Coleman Barks)

The Piano & Piano Lessons

Bill Holm

from PLAYING HAYDN
FOR THE ANGEL OF DEATH

The piano tells things to your hands
you never let yourself hear from others:
Calm down, do your work, laugh,
love reason more, your mask less.
God exists, though not as church said.
To understand this language, you must
sometimes patiently play the same
piece over and over for years, then
when you expect nothing, the music
lets go its wisdom.

Howard Nemerov

To His Piano

Old friend, patient of error as of accuracy,
Ready to think the fingerings of thought,
You but a scant year older than I am
With my expectant mother expecting maybe
An infant prodigy among her stars
But getting only little me instead—

To see you standing there for six decades
Containing Chopsticks, Für Elise, and
The Art of Fugue in your burnished rosewood box,
As well as all those years of silence and
The stumbling beginnings the children made,
Who would believe the twenty tons of stress
Your gilded frame's kept stretched out all this while?

Dorianne Laux

THE EBONY CHICKERING

My mother cooked with lard she kept
In coffee cans beneath the kitchen sink.
Bean-colored linoleum ticked under her flats
as she wore a path from stove to countertop.
Eggs cracked against the lips of smooth
ceramic bowls she beat muffins in,
boxed cakes and cookie dough.
It was the afternoons she worked toward,
the smell of onions scrubbed from her hands,
when she would fold her flowered apron
and feed it through the sticky refrigerator
handle, adjust the spongy curlers on her head
and wrap a loud Hawaiian scarf into a tired knot
around them as she walked toward her piano,
the one thing my father had given her that she loved.
I can still see each gold letter engraved
on the polished lid she lifted and slid
into the piano's dark body, the hidden hammers
trembling like a muffled word,
the scribbled sheets, her rough hands poised
above the keys as she began her daily practice.
Words like *arpeggio* sparkled through my childhood,
her fingers sliding from the black bar of a sharp
to the white of a common note. "This is Bach,"
she would instruct us, the tail of his name hissing
like a cat. "And Chopin," she said, "was French,
like us," pointing to the sheet music. "Listen.
Don't let the letters fool you. It's best
to always trust your ear."

She played parts of fugues and lost concertos,
played hard as we kicked each other on the couch,
while the meat burned and the wet wash wrinkled
in the basket, played Beethoven as if she understood
the caged world of the deaf, his terrible music
pounding its way through the fence slats
and the screened doors of the cul-de-sac, the yards
where other mothers hung clothes on a wire, bent
to weeds, swept the driveways clean.
Those were the years she taught us how to make
quick easy meals, accept the embarrassment
of a messy house, safety pins and rick-rack
hanging from the hem of her dress.
But I knew the other kids didn't own words
like *fortissimo* and *mordant, treble clef*
and *trill*, or have a mother quite as elegant
as mine when she sat at the piano,
playing like she was famous,
so that when the Sparklets man arrived
to fill our water cooler every week
he would lean against the doorjamb and wait
for her to finish, glossy-eyed
as he listened, secretly touching the tips
of his fingers to the tips of her fingers
as he bowed, and she slipped him the check.

John Hollander

KRANICH AND BACH
A BRAND OF PIANO NO LONGER MADE

Under her golden willow a golden crane
Hangs over golden water, stencilled on the
Heavy lamplit brown of the solemn upright:

Silence standing in a pool of reflection?
Or, if the brook's waters rumble darkly on,
Silence reflecting by a flow of music?

No golden harp with golden wires depends from
The vaulted branch on the shiny varnished ground,
Mirroring the ebony and ivory,

And the glint of golden from a wedding-band,
And the earnest hands of my poor father, who
With forgotten fingers played as best he could,

Muttering, or even roaring out the texts:
Erl-King strokes the boy; trout die in their now-dulled
Stream; the wan Double carries on in moonlight;

Impatience stutters on the keys; water turns
Through its rippling figures, and always the old
Man, bare amid a few tattered chords, still stands

Grinding out his music, *dyum de dum dum dum:*
"Both his feet are bare upon the frozen ground,
In his empty saucer no coin makes a sound."

Lyre-man, I would not know for years that you
Stand at the end of a journey of winter
To be followed only into its silence

As I will follow my father into his.
Dark under the closed lid, Kranich and Bach wait,
Silence standing up one-leggedly in song.

D. H. Lawrence

PIANO

Softly, in the dusk, a woman is singing to me;
Taking me back down the vista of years, till I see
A child sitting under the piano, in the boom of the tingling
    strings
And pressing the small, poised feet of a mother who smiles as
    she sings.

In spite of myself, the insidious mastery of song
Betrays me back, till the heart of me weeps to belong
To the old Sunday evenings at home, with winter outside
And hymns in the cosy parlour, the tinkling piano our guide.

So now it is vain for the singer to burst into clamour
With the great black piano appassionato. The glamour
Of childish days is upon me, my manhood is cast
Down in the flood of remembrance, I weep like a child for the
    past.

Donald Justice

VARIATIONS FOR TWO PIANOS

For Thomas Higgins, pianist

There is no music now in all Arkansas.
Higgins is gone, taking both his pianos.

Movers dismantled the instruments, away
Sped the vans; the first detour untuned the strings.

There is no music now in all Arkansas.

Up Main Street, past the cold shopfronts of Conway,
The brash, self-important brick of the college,

Higgins is gone, taking both his pianos.

Warm evenings, the windows open, he would play
Something of Mozart's for his pupils, the birds.

There is no music now in all Arkansas.

How shall the mockingbird mend her trill, the jay
His eccentric attack, lacking a teacher?

Higgins is gone, taking both his pianos.
There is no music now in all Arkansas.

Wallace Stevens

PIANO PRACTICE AT THE ACADEMY OF THE HOLY ANGELS

The time will come for these children, seated before their long
    black instruments, to strike the themes of love—
All of them, darkened by time, moved by they know not what,
    amending the airs they play to fulfill themselves;
Seated before these shining forms, like the duskiest glass, re-
    flecting the piebald of roses or what you will.
Blanche, the blonde, whose eyes are not wholly straight in a
    room of lustres, shed by turquoise falling,
Whose heart will murmur with the music that will be a voice for
    her, speaking the dreaded change of speech;
And Rosa, the muslin dreamer of satin and cowry-kin, disdaining
    the empty keys; and the young infanta,
Jocunda, who will arrange the roses and rearrange, letting the
    leaves lie on the water-like lacquer;
And that confident one, Marie, the wearer of cheap stones, who
    will have grown still and restless;
And Chrispine, the blade, reddened by some touch, demanding
    the most from the phrases
Of the well-thumbed, infinite pages of her masters, who will seem
    old to her, requiting less and less her feeling:
In the days when the mood of love will be swarming for solace
    and sink deeply into the thin stuff of being,
And these long, black instruments will be so little to them that
    will be needing so much, seeking so much in their music.

Ogden Nash

PIANO TUNER,
UNTUNE ME THAT TUNE

I regret that before people can be reformed they have to be
    sinners,
And that before you have pianists in the family you have
    to have beginners.
When it comes to beginners' music
I am not enthusic.
When listening to something called "An Evening in My Doll
    House," or "Buzz, Buzz, Said the Bee to the Clover,"
Why I'd like just once to hear it played all the way through,
    instead of that hard part near the end over and over.
Have you noticed about little fingers?
When they hit a sour note, they lingers.
And another thing about little fingers, they are always
    strawberry-jammed or cranberry-jellied-y,
And "Chopsticks" is their favorite melody,
And if there is one man who I hope his dentist was a
    sadist and all his teeth were brittle ones,
It is he who invented "Chopsticks" for the little ones.
My good wishes are less than frugal
For him who started the little ones going boogie-woogal,
But for him who started the little ones picking out
    "Chopsticks" on the ivories,
Well I wish him a thousand harems of a thousand wives
    apiece, and a thousand little ones by each wife, and each
    little one playing "chopsticks" twenty-four hours a day
    in all the nurseries of all his harems, or wiveries.

Valerie Gillies

THE PIANO TUNER

Two hundred miles, he had come
    to tune one piano, the last hereabouts.
Both of them were relics of imperial time:
    the Anglo-Indian and the old upright knock-about.

He peered, and peered again
    into its monsoon-warped bowels.
From the flats of dead sound he'd beckon
    a tune on the bones out to damp vowels.

His own sounds were pidgin.
    The shapeliness of his forearms
lent his body an English configuration,
    but still, sallow as any snakecharmer

he was altogether piebald.
    Far down the bridge of his nose
perched roundrimmed tortoiseshell spectacles;
    his hair, a salt-and-pepper, white foreclosed.

But he rings in the ear yet,
    his interminable tapping of jarring notes:
and, before he left,
    he gave point to those hours of discord.

With a smile heavenly
    because so out of place, cut off from any home there,
he sat down quietly
    to play soft music: that tune of 'Beautiful Dreamer',

a melody seized from yellowed ivories
　　and rotting wood. A damper
muffled the pedal point of lost birthright. We eaves-
　　dropped on an extinct creature.

Billy Collins

Piano Lessons

1

My teacher lies on the floor with a bad back
off to the side of the piano.
I sit up straight on the stool.
He begins by telling me that every key
is like a different room
and I am a blind man who must learn
to walk through all twelve of them
without hitting the furniture.
I feel myself reach for the first doorknob.

2

He tells me that every scale has a shape
and I have to learn how to hold
each one in my hands.
At home I practice with my eyes closed.
C is an open book.
D is a vase with two handles.
G flat is a black boot.
E has the legs of a bird.

3

He says the scale is the mother of the chords.
I can see her pacing the bedroom floor
waiting for her children to come home.
They are out at nightclubs shading and lighting
all the songs while couples dance slowly

or stare at one another across tables.
This is the way it must be. After all,
just the right chord can bring you to tears
but no one listens to the scales,
no one listens to their mother.

4

I am doing my scales,
the familiar anthems of childhood.
My fingers climb the ladder of notes
and come back down without turning around.
Anyone walking under this open window
would picture a girl of about ten
sitting at the keyboard with perfect posture,
not me slumped over in my bathrobe, disheveled,
like a white Horace Silver.

5

I am learning to play
"It Might As Well Be Spring"
but my left hand would rather be jingling
the change in the darkness of my pocket
or taking a nap on an armrest.
I have to drag him into the music
like a difficult and neglected child.
This is the revenge of the one who never gets
to hold the pen or wave good-bye,
and now, who never gets to play the melody.

6

Even when I am not playing, I think about the piano.
It is the largest, heaviest,
and most beautiful object in this house.
I pause in the doorway just to take it all in.
And late at night I picture it downstairs,
this hallucination standing on three legs,
this curious beast with its enormous moonlit smile.

Donald Justice

THE PUPIL

Picture me, the shy pupil at the door,
One small, tight fist clutching the dread Czerny.
Back then time was still harmony, not money,
And I could spend a whole week practicing for
That moment on the threshold.
                                   Then to take courage,
And enter, and pass among mysterious scents,
And sit quite straight, and with a frail confidence
Assault the keyboard with a childish flourish!

Only to lose my place, or forget the key,
And almost doubt the very metronome
(Outside, the traffic, the laborers going home),
And still to bear on across Chopin or Brahms,
Stupid and wild with love equally for the storms
Of C# minor and the calms of C.

Linda Pastan

PRACTICING

My son is practicing the piano.
He is a man now, not the boy
whose lessons I once sat through,
whose reluctant practicing
I demanded—part of the obligation
I felt to the growth
and composition of a child.

Upstairs my grandchildren are sleeping,
though they complained earlier of the music
which rises like smoke up through the floorboards,
coloring the fabric of their dreams.
On the porch my husband watches the garden fade
into summer twilight, flower by flower;
it must be a little like listening to the fading

diminuendo notes of Mozart.
But here where the dining room table
has been pushed aside to make room
for this second or third-hand upright,
my son is playing the kind of music
it took him all these years,
and sons of his own, to want to make.

Brigit Pegeen Kelly

THE MUSIC LESSON

Collect of white dusk. And
The first epistolary drops
Strike sparks from the leaves,

Send up the sweet fragrance
Of the Far Gone. Where
The maple fell in another rain

Red and white umbrellas
Hold back the weather: sun
And moon and the seasonal

Displays the four hands
Keep time to: the telling
And the told. Back and forth:

Back and forth: the lesson's
Passion is patience. Through
The domino tumble and clutter

Of the pupil's untutored touch
The metronome keeps
A stiff upper lip, pays out

Its narrow train of thought
While above, God,
Gold carrion in a lit frame,

Rehearses His reproach, one-
Noted. Final. The unnegotiable
Real estate of absolute loss:

Discipleship's cost. O hands,
Hands, doing their work:
The steeple hat of the dunce

Is stiff with recalcitrant
Notes, but still the ghost hammers
Leap. And luck makes an entrance

In this: See: lightning
Partitions the dusk—illuminating
Our brief lease—and with

A cocksure infusion of heat
Luck lays hands on
The boy's hands and prefigures

The pleasure that will one day
Possess this picture for good.
This is the stone the builders

Rejected. Pleasure. *Pleasure.*
The liquid tool, the golden
Fossil that will come to fuel

In lavish and unspeakable ways
All the dry passages
The boy does not now comprehend

Or care for. And then his
Stricken hands will blossom
Fat with brag. And play.

Adam Zagajewski

DEATH OF A PIANIST

While others waged war
or sued for peace, or lay
in narrow beds in hospitals
or camps, for days on end

he practiced Beethoven's sonatas,
and slim fingers, like a miser's,
touched great treasures
that weren't his.

Muriel Rukeyser

GRADUS AD PARNASSUM

Oh I know
If I'd practiced the piano
I'd never be so low
As I now am

Where's Sylvia Beerman?
Married, rich and cool
In New Rochelle
She was nobody's fool,

She didn't write in verse
She hardly wrote at all
She rose she didn't fall
She never gave a damn

But got up early
To practise Gradus
Ad Parnassum—she
Feels fine. I know.

Fleur Adcock

Piano Concerto in E Flat Major

In her 1930s bob or even, perhaps,
if she saw something quainter as her fashion,
long thick hair in a plait, the music student
showed her composition to her tutor;
and she aroused, or this enhanced, his passion.

He quoted from it in his new concerto,
offering back to her as homage
those several bars of hers the pianist plays
in the second movement: part of what she dreamed
re-translated, marked more with his image.

But the seven steady notes of the main theme
are his alone. Did the romance go well?
Whether he married her's recorded somewhere
in books. The wistful strings, the determined
percussion, the English cadences, don't tell.

William Jay Smith

WOMAN AT THE PIANO

When the tall thin lady started to play
the notes flew up and out and away:
like the pink in her cheeks and her dress's loops
they rose in curves, they rolled in hoops
till the chickens flew out of the chicken coops,
the rooster crowed, the donkey brayed,
and the cat meowed.

She raised her hands,

she lifted her feet.

What was she playing?

An anthem? A hymn?

Nobody knew, but oh, it was sweet!

How thin she was, how tall and prim,

but, oh, how she played!

Everything in you went loose inside
and the world of a sudden became so wide
and open and joyous and free
the fish came flying out of the sea,
the mountains knelt,

the birds went wild.

The lady smiled:

and all you could do was hold on to your seat
and simply say:

"For heaven's sake, lady, play, play!
for heaven's sake,
                lady,
                        play!"

Robert Frost

THE INVESTMENT

Over back where they speak of life as staying
("You couldn't call it living, for it ain't"),
There was an old, old house renewed with paint,
And in it a piano loudly playing.

Out in the plowed ground in the cold a digger,
Among unearthed potatoes standing still,
Was counting winter dinners, one a hill,
With half an ear to the piano's vigor.

All that piano and new paint back there,
Was it some money suddenly come into?
Or some extravagance young love had been to?
Or old love on an impulse not to care—

Not to sink under being man and wife,
But get some color and music out of life?

Kenneth Weisner

UNDER THE PIANO

For Kit

There is nothing better than listening
to Debussy's Claire de Lune,
under your piano.
Students who are leaving you
go under their last day
and listen to you
play for them.
It's how you say goodbye.

The piano sits in the corner
of the small carpeted front room,
a Baldwin baby grand
next to my Grandmother's hundred-year-old
German side table with lions' paws.
You have them dive right back there
into the dark corner
beneath the bass strings. In a way,

a piano is a horrifying thing;
this black angel's coffin
could come thumping down
and kill someone.
You and a student rode it out there
during the big quake;
a bookshelf full of music
smashed the bench,
stopping inches from the keys.

When I arrived home yesterday,
you were playing Rachmaninoff's Prelude in G Minor.
I don't know why—I didn't even break stride—
just went right under
to close my eyes awhile
after a long day.

I love this part . . . a dramatic downward run
proclaims its minor key, some triumph in exile, turned
sumptuous, rising back upwards now. . . .

And though I am not your student,
and you are not saying goodbye,
how good it is that you are playing
now for me! sprawled on the old carpet
appreciating every heady consonance
but also every jangly overtone
and percussive distortion,
the hilarious volume and vivid harmonics;
no, not even a kiss can do this.
And as in love,
even the mistakes are glorious,
blunt thunder.

And then when you go a long time without missing a
note,
how marvelous—what a miracle—
transported by virtuosity

into the composer's heart, or is it your heart?
or is it my own?
Oh, terrible exile;
wonderful life.

And such a private place, sacred: the piano
filling the sky.
So the wonder
mixes with the love, music, and privacy
to form
shameless ecstasy,
a fortune so difficult to find these days
in nature, the Church, politics
or even the theater.

It may not be God, but I feel loved,
you feel loved.
All the better because neither
the machine nor the interpreter
is perfect,
but the resulting chaos might be
the best thing in life.

And having married the piano player
many stormy years ago,
now, without sentimentality but in
the presence of
Rachmaninoff—
so much meaning—
and hearing the wonderful sense

in the sound, mouth set in its slight smirk,
so used to being disappointed at the world . . .
I for once do the logical thing:
nothing—just lie there
and weep through the whole recap and coda,
silently, shamelessly, for the ecstasy of it.

Derek Walcott

PIANO PRACTICE

For Mark Strand

April, in another fortnight, metropolitan April.
A drizzle glazes the museum's entrance,
like their eyes when they leave you, equivocating spring!
The sun dries the avenue's pumice façade
delicately as a girl tamps tissue on her cheek;
the asphalt shines like a silk hat,
the fountains trot like percherons round the Met,
clip, clop, clip, clop in Belle Epoque Manhattan,
as gutters part their lips to the spring rain—
down avenues hazy as Impressionist clichés,
their gargoyle cornices,
their concrete flowers on chipped pediments,
their subway stops in Byzantine mosaic—
the soul sneezes and one tries to compile
the collage of a closing century,
the epistolary pathos, the old Laforguean ache.

Deserted plazas swept by gusts of remorse,
rain-polished cobbles where a curtained carriage
trotted around a corner of Europe for the last time,
as the canals folded like concertinas.
Now fever reddens the trouble spots of the globe,
rain drizzles on the white iron chairs in the gardens.

Today is Thursday, Vallejo is dying,
but come, girl, get your raincoat, let's look for life
in some café behind tear-streaked windows,
perhaps the *fin de siècle* isn't really finished,

maybe there's a piano playing it somewhere,
as the bulbs burn through the heart of the afternoon
in the season of tulips and the pale assassin.
I called the Muse, she pleaded a headache,
but maybe she was just shy at being seen
with someone who has only one climate,
so I passed the flowers in stone, the sylvan pediments,
alone. It wasn't I who shot the archduke,
I excuse myself of all crimes of that ilk,
muttering the subway's obscene graffiti;
I could offer her nothing but the predictable
pale head-scarf of the twilight's lurid silk.

Well, goodbye, then, I'm sorry I've never gone
to the great city that gave Vallejo fever.
Maybe the Seine outshines the East River,
maybe, but near the Metropolitan
a steel tenor pan
dazzlingly practices something from old Vienna,
the scales skittering like minnows across the sea.

Horns, Woodwinds, & Strings

Robert Phillips

INSTRUMENT OF CHOICE

She was a girl
no one ever chose
for teams or clubs,
dances or dates,

so she chose the instrument
no one else wanted:
the tuba. Big as herself,
heavy as her heart,

its golden tubes
and coils encircled her
like a lover's embrace.
Its body pressed on hers.

Into its mouthpiece she blew
life, its deep-throated
oompahs, oompahs sounding,
almost, like mating cries.

John Updike

RECITAL

ROGER BOBO GIVES RECITAL ON TUBA
        —*headline in the* New York Times

Eskimos in Manitoba,
        Barracuda off Aruba,
Cock an ear when Roger Bobo
        Starts to solo on the tuba.

Men of every station—Pooh-Bah
        Nabob, bozo, toff, and hobo—
Cry in unison, "Indubi-
        Tably, there is simply nobo-

Dy who oompahs on the tubo,
Solo, quite like Rober Bubo!"

Robert Pinsky

GINZA SAMBA

A monosyllabic European called Sax
Invents a horn, walla whirledy wah, a kind of twisted
Brazen clarinet, but with its column of vibrating
Air shaped not in a cylinder but in a cone
Widening ever outward and bawaah spouting
Infinitely upward through an upturned
Swollen golden bell rimmed
Like a gloxinia flowering
In Sax's Belgian imagination

And in the unfathomable matrix
Of mothers and fathers as a genius graven
Humming into the cells of the body
Or cupped in the resonating grail
Of memory changed and exchanged
As in the trading of brasses,
Pearls and ivory, calicos and slaves,
Laborers and girls, two

Cousins in a royal family
Of Niger known as the Birds or Hawks.
In Christendom one cousin's child
Becomes a "favorite negro" ennobled
By decree of the Czar and founds
A great family, a line of generals,
Dandies and courtiers including the poet
Pushkin, killed in a duel concerning
His wife's honor, while the other cousin sails

In the belly of a slaveship to the port
Of Baltimore where she is raped
And dies in childbirth, but the infant
Will marry a Seminole and in the next
Chorus of time their child fathers
A great Hawk or Bird, with many followers
Among them this great-grandchild of the Jewish
Manager of a Pushkin estate, blowing

His American breath out into the wiggly
Tune uncurling its triplets and sixteenths—the Ginza
Samba of breath and brass, the reed
Vibrating as a valve, the aether, the unimaginable
Wires and circuits of an ingenious box
Here in my room in this house built
A hundred years ago while I was elsewhere:

It is like falling in love, the atavistic
Imperative of some one
Voice or face—the skill, the copper filament,
The golden bellful of notes twirling through
Their invisible element from
Rio to Tokyo and back again gathering
Speed in the variations as they tunnel
The twin haunted labyrinths of stirrup
And anvil echoing here in the hearkening
Instrument of my skull.

Kenneth Fields

A BELACQUA B FLAT TRUMPET

A sylph kissing the shaft of the mouthpiece furls
Along the curves and casings, airy breath,
The sudden graven plumage of great desire
Flaring to a fine Chimera round the bell,
The two mouths drawing water into air,
One fiery exaltation. The old man makes
Fewer than ten a year. He hears them all,
The visible ones, and the invisible,
Their flagged and dotted runs, the dark glow
Of the legato lags, the bravura swell . . .
All brass at the last day. May it never come,
At least not now, he thinks. With such a horn,
Warmed by the respiration of the soul,
Purgatory itself is Paradise.

Eugenio Montale

English Horn

The intent wind that plays tonight
—recalling a sharp clash of metal sheets—
the instruments of the thick trees and sweeps
the copper horizon
where streaks of light are trailing,
kites in the sky that roars
(traveling clouds, bright
kingdoms up above,
High Eldorados' half-shut doors!)
and the livid sea
which, scale by scale,
turns color, hurls
a horn of contorted spume ashore;
the wind that's born and dies
in the hour that slowly goes dark—
if only it could play you, too, tonight,
discordant instrument,
heart.

(Translated by Jonathan Galassi)

W. S. Merwin

THE NOMAD FLUTE

You that sang to me once sing to me now
let me hear your long lifted note
survive with me
the star is fading
I can think farther than that but I forget
do you hear me

do you still hear me
does your air
remember me
oh breath of morning
night song morning song
I have with me
all that I do not know
I have lost none of it

but I know better now
than to ask you
where you learned that music
where any of it came from
once there were lions in China

I will listen until the flute stops
and the light is old again

Mina Loy

STRAVINSKI'S FLUTE

The swan's neck stiffens
and the swan
starts from the swamps of Silence

A voice-evangel of loud ice
soars through a cloven dome

Elysian whistler
trailing a strand of sound
to fluted altitude

as from a Hindu's hand is flung
a rope into Nirvana

Arise
shrill star-striker—

To this listening
the mouth and the ear
of music
are one

Carol Muske-Dukes

CONCERTINA

The air is filled with unfriendly music.
In the street, I am confronted by three angry instruments:
a mandolin and two furious cellos.
They are fed up with my indifference,
this preoccupation with my own dissonance.
They shriek and pluck the strings across their hearts,
                          in attitudes of despair.

Later they invite me for sherry in a bordello
and try to reason with me,
weeping white gloves, noting repeatedly my resemblance
to a harpsichord. I spy a fortune teller
across the room, staring at herself in an hourglass
humming patriotic ballads.

In my palm she sees a long voyage
into a tall dark piano.
She kneels and kisses my ears.
The music begins to drive me mad.

I take her advice
and leave by a side door
pursued by the sound of flutes.

Louise Bogan

MUSICIAN

Where have these hands been,
By what delayed,
That so long stayed
Apart from the thin

Strings which they now grace
With their lonely skill?
Music and their cool will
At last interlace.

Now with great ease, and slow,
The thumb, the finger, the strong
Delicate hand plucks the long
String it was born to know.

And, under the palm, the string
Sings as it wished to sing.

May Sarton

GIRL WITH 'CELLO

There had been no such music here until
A girl came in from falling dark and snow
To bring into this house her glowing 'cello
As if some silent, magic animal.

She sat, head bent, her long hair all a-spill
Over the breathing wood, and drew the bow.
There had been no such music here until
A girl came in from falling dark and snow.

And she drew out that sound so like a wail,
A rich dark suffering joy, as if to show
All that a wrist holds and that fingers know
When they caress a magic animal.
There had been no such music here until
A girl came in from falling dark and snow.

Galway Kinnell

THE CELLIST

At intermission I find her backstage
still practicing the piece coming up next.
She calls it the "solo in high dreary."
Her bow niggles at the strings like a hand
stroking skin it never wanted to touch.
Probably under her scorn she is sick
that she can't do better by it. As I am,
by the dreary in me, such as the disparity
between all the tenderness I've received
and the amount I've given, and the way
I used to shrug off the imbalance
simply as how things are, as if the male
were constituted like those coffeemakers
that produce less black bitter than the quantity
of sweet clear you pour in—forgetting about
how much I spilled through unsteady walking,
and that lot I flung on the ground
in suspicion, and for fear I wasn't worthy,
and all I threw out for reasons I don't understand yet.
"Break a leg!" somebody tells her.
Back in my seat, I can see she is nervous
when she comes out; her hand shakes as she
re-dog-ears the top corners of the big pages
that look about to flop over on their own.
Now she raises the bow—its flat bundle of hair
harvested from the rear ends of horses—like a whetted
scimitar she is about to draw across a throat,
and attacks. In a back alley a cat opens
its pink-ceilinged mouth, gets netted
in full yowl, clubbed, bagged, bicycled off, haggled open,

gutted, the gut squeezed down to its highest pitch,
washed, and sliced into cello strings that bring
a screaming into this duet of hair and gut.
Now she is flying—tossing back the goblets
of Saint-Amour standing empty,
half-empty, or full on the tablecloth-
like sheet music. Her knees tighten
and loosen around the big-hipped creature
wailing and groaning between them
as if locked with her in syzygial amplexus.
The music seems to rise from the crater left
when heaven was torn up and taken out of the earth;
more likely it comes up through her priest's dress
up from beneath that clump of hair which by now
may be so wet with its waters, miraculous as the waters
the fishes multiplied in at Galilee, that
each strand wicks a portion all the way out
to its tip and fattens a droplet on the bush
of half notes now glittering in that dark.
At last she lifts off the bow and sits back.
Her face shines with the unselfconsciousness of a cat
screaming at night and the teary radiance of one
who gives everything no matter what has been given.

Carl Rakosi

INSTRUCTIONS TO THE PLAYER

Cellist,
        easy on that bow.
Not too much weeping.

Remember that the soul
              is easily agitated
and has a terror of shapelessness.
It will venture out
          but only to a doe's eye.

Let the sound out
          inner *misterioso*
but from a distance
          like the forest at night.

And do not forget
          the pause between.
That is the sweetest
and has the nature of infinity.

Linda Pastan

BEETHOVEN'S QUARTET IN C MAJOR, OPUS 59

The violins
are passionately
occupied, but
it is the cellist

who seems to be
holding the music
in his arms,
moving his bow

as if it were
a dowsing rod
and the audience
dying of thirst.

Naomi Shihab Nye

VIOLIN

It's been sleeping under the bed
for twenty years.

Once I let it out every day.
Neighbors picked up bits of music
wedged into grass.

I stroked the resiny hairs of bow.
All my tutors, lunatics, but my mother
left us alone.

Sometimes a sonata
broke in the middle—
I stitched it together
slowly, slowly.

Graceful shoulders,
elegant neck—
what do you know now
that you didn't know then?

Rolf Jacobsen

HAYDN

In the great Haydn concerto
where the violins were hosannas to heaven
and the harps the deep heartbeats of creation,
her fingers across the bronze strings
were the dance of butterflies
as they unfolded and closed,
unfolded,
unfolded and closed
like moth wings translucent with frost,
fluttering, fluttering
at the large window that never opens,
outside the glass, outside the glass
and never inside.

(Translated by Robert Hedin)

Pablo Neruda

From ODE TO THE GUITAR

Slender,
            perfect profile
of a musical heart,
you are clarity itself captured in flight.
Through song you endure:
your shape alone will never pass away...

———•··•———

Time and distance
fall away from the guitar.
We are a dream,
an unfinished
song.
The untamed heart
rides back roads on horseback:
over and over again it dreams of the night, of silence,
over and over again it sings of the earth, of its guitar.

(Translated by Ken Krabbenhoft)

Federico García Lorca

THE GUITAR

The guitar
begins its weeping.
The wineglasses of dawn
are shattered.
The guitar
begins its weeping.
It is useless
to hush it.
Impossible
to hush it.
It cries monotonously,
as the water cries,
as the wind cries
over the snowfield.
It is impossible
to hush it.
It cries
for distant things.
Sand from the hot South
asking for white camellias.
It cries, arrow with no target,
evening with no morning,
and the first bird
dead on the branch.
Oh guitar!
Heart mortally wounded
by five swords.

(Translated by Christopher Maurer)

Louise Labé

THE TWELFTH SONNET

My lute, my sole companion in distress,
Silent and grave attendant to my tears,
Witness of my affections and my fears,
Echo to all my love and loneliness:

I have so hindered you with all this folly
That now, if it occurs to me to play
Some clearer note, it quickly falls away
Into a minor chord; your melancholy

Echoes, persists. And if I try again,
The sound is subtly altered and the string
Slackens, is mute. And only lamentation

Draws a response from you. In suffering
Alone you bring your music; and the strain
Of loveliness is found in desolation.

(*Translated by Frederic Prokosch*)

Composers

Lars Gustafsson

THE STILLNESS OF THE WORLD BEFORE BACH

There must have been a world before
the Trio Sonata in D, a world before the A minor Partita,
but what kind of a world?
A Europe of vast empty spaces, unresounding,
everywhere unawakened instruments
where the *Musical Offering*, the *Well-tempered Clavier*
never passed across the keys.
Isolated churches
where the soprano line of the *Passion*
never in helpless love twined round
the gentler movements of the flute,
broad soft landscapes
where nothing breaks the stillness
but old woodcutters' axes,
the healthy barking of strong dogs in winter
and, like a bell, skates biting into fresh ice;
the swallows whirring through summer air,
the shell resounding at the child's ear
and nowhere Bach nowhere Bach
the world in a skater's stillness before Bach.

(Translated by Philip Martin)

Charles Tomlinson

IF BACH HAD BEEN A BEEKEEPER

If Bach had been a beekeeper
he would have heard
all those notes
suspended above one another
in the air of his ear
as the differentiated swarm returning
to the exact hive,
and place in the hive,
topping up the cells
with the honey of C major,
food for the listening generations,
key to their comfort
and solace of their distress
as they return and return
to those counterpointed levels
of hovering wings where
movement is dance
and the air itself
a scented garden

Dana Gioia

GOD ONLY KNOWS

Here is the church,
Here is the steeple,
Open it up,
And see all the people.

God only knows

if Bach's greatest work
was just an improvised
accompaniment
between two verses of a hymn,
one that stopped the burghers
squirming in their pews
and made them not only
listen to the organ in the loft
but actually hear the roof
unbend itself
and leave the church wide
open to a terrifying sky
which he had filled with angels
holding ledgers
for a roll call of the damned,
whom they would have named,
had not the congregation
started up the final chorus
and sung

to save their souls.

Howard Nemerov

from PLAYING THE INVENTIONS

Landowska said, to end an argument,
"Why don't you go on playing Bach your way
and let me play Bach his way?" putting down
Whoever-it-was forever; music's not
All harmony, Landowska too is dead,
Spirit acerb, though her records remain
Hermetically kept where time not much corrupts
Nor quite so quick. In our advancing age
Not only the effigy can be preserved
But the sound as well, only without the self,
As evanescent as it ever was.
At last even the inventions lock us out,
We go while they remain. The argument ends.
It's like a myth about inventing death:
We don't become immortal, but it does.

———

Ach, dear Bach, so beautiful a day!
A small breeze shakes the shadows of the leaves
Over the instrument, across your page,
Sprinklings of drops at the outer edge of spray
In patterns overpatterning your own.
And one sits here, "lover of the clavier
And desirous to learn," your backward dilettante,
Amateur, stumbling slowly through your thoughts
Where five and twenty decades of the world's
Sorrow and wrath are for a while as though

Dissolved in the clear streams of your songs
Whose currents twine, diverge, and twine again,
Seeming to think themselves about themselves
Like fountains flowering in their fall. Dear Bach,
It's a great privilege. It always is.

Delmore Schwartz

from VIVALDI

The music declares
"Is this what you want? Is this the good news for which you
      have been here convened—
To be, to become, and to participate in the sweet congress of
      serene attention,
Silent, attentive, motionless, waiting,
Save for the heart clutching itself and the hushed breathing?"
The answered question is: Our being. Our presence. Our
      surrender.
Consciousness has consented, is consumed, has surrendered,
      to hear only the players playing.
Consciousness has become only and purely listening.

     The vivid world has been barred,
     The press of desire shut out.
This is the dark city of the innermost wish,
     The motion beyond emotion,
     The power beyond and free of power.
This is the dark city of the hidden innermost wish,
This is the immortality of mortality, this
Is supreme consciousness, the grasped reality of reality,
moving
     forward,
     Now and forever.

Tomas Tranströmer

ALLEGRO

After a black day, I play Haydn,
and feel a little warmth in my hands.

The keys are ready. Kind hammers fall.
The sound is spirited, green, and full of silence.

The sound says that freedom exists
and someone pays no taxes to Caesar.

I shove my hands in my haydnpockets
and act like a man who is calm about it all.

I raise my haydnflag. The signal is:
"We do not surrender. But want peace."

The music is a house of glass standing on a slope;
rocks are flying, rocks are rolling.

The rocks roll straight through the house
but every pane of glass is still whole.

(*Translated by Robert Bly*)

Edgar Bowers

From J. Haydn to Constanze Mozart (1791)

Incredibly near the vital edge of tears,
I write, Constanze, having heard our loss.
Only the shape of memory adheres
To the most nearly perfect human pose
I hope to find, though mind and heart grow fierce,
Five times again as fierce as his repose.

The mind of most of us is trivial;
The heart is moved too quickly and too much.
He thought each movement that was animal,
And senses were the mind's continual search
To find the perfect note, emotional
And mental, each the other one's reproach.

With him as master, grief should be serene,
Death its own joy, and joy opposed by death,
What is made living by what should have been,
And understanding constant in its wrath
Within one life to fix them both the same,
Though no one can, unless it be in death.

Yet we who loved him have that right to mourn.
Let this be mine, that fastened on my eyes
I carry one small memory of his form
Aslant at his clavier, with careful ease,
To bring one last enigma to the norm,
Intelligence perfecting the mute keys.

Mary Oliver

MOZART, FOR EXAMPLE

All the quick notes
Mozart didn't have time to use
before he entered the cloud-boat

are falling now from the beaks
of the finches
that have gathered from the joyous summer

into the hard winter
and, like Mozart, they speak of nothing
but light and delight,

though it is true, the heavy blades of the world
are still pounding underneath.
And this is what you can do too, maybe,

if you live simply and with a lyrical heart
in the cumbered neighborhoods or even,
as Mozart sometimes managed to, in a palace,

offering tune after tune after tune,
making some hard-hearted prince
prudent and kind, just by being happy.

Leonard Cohen

HIS MASTER'S VOICE

After listening to Mozart
(which I often did)
I would always
Carry a piano
Up and down
Mt. Baldy
And I don't mean
A keyboard
I mean a full-sized
Grand piano
Made of cement
Now that I am dying
I don't regret
A single step

Dana Gioia

LIVES OF THE GREAT COMPOSERS

Herr Bruckner often wandered into church
to join the mourners at a funeral.
The relatives of Berlioz were horrified.
"Such harmony," quoth Shakespeare, "is in
immortal souls.... We cannot hear it." But
the radio is playing, and outside
rain splashes to the pavement. Now and then
the broadcast fails. On nights like these Schumann
would watch the lightning streak his windowpanes.

Outside the rain is falling on the pavement.
A scrap of paper tumbles down the street.
On rainy evenings Schumann jotted down
his melodies on windowpanes. "Such harmony!
We cannot hear it." The radio goes off and on.
At the rehearsal Gustav Holst exclaimed,
"I'm sick of music, especially my own!"
The relatives of Berlioz were horrified.
Haydn's wife used music to line pastry pans.

On rainy nights the ghost of Mendelssohn
brought melodies for Schumann to compose.
"Such harmony is in immortal souls....
We cannot hear it." One could suppose
Herr Bruckner would have smiled. At Tergensee
the peasants stood to hear young Paganini play,
but here there's lightning, and the thunder rolls.
The radio goes off and on. The rain
falls to the pavement like applause.

A scrap of paper tumbles down the street.
On rainy evenings Schumann would look out
and scribble on the windows of his cell.
"Such harmony." Cars splash out in the rain.
The relatives of Berlioz were horrified
to see the horses break from the cortege
and gallop with his casket to the grave.
Liszt wept to hear young Paganini play.
Haydn's wife used music to line pastry pans.

Adam Zagajewski

LATE BEETHOVEN

I haven't yet known a man who loved virtue as
strongly as one loves beauty.   —Confucius

Nobody knows who she was, the Immortal
Beloved. Apart from that, everything is
clear. Feathery notes rest
peacefully on the threads of the staff
like martins just come
from the Atlantic. What would I have to be
in order to speak about him, he who's still
growing. Now we are walking alone
without ghosts or banners. Long live
chaos, say our solitary mouths.
We know that he dressed carelessly,
that he was given to fits of avarice, that he wasn't
always fair to his friends.
Friends are a hundred years
late with their impeccable smiles. Who
was the Immortal Beloved? Certainly,
he loved virtue more than beauty.
But a nameless god of beauty dwelled
in him and compelled his obedience.
He improvised for hours. A few minutes
of each improvisation were noted down.
These minutes belong neither to the nineteenth
nor to the twentieth century; as if hydrochloric
acid burned a window in velvet, thus
opening a passage to even
smoother velvet, thin as
a spiderweb. Now they name

ships and perfumes after him. They don't know who
the Immortal Beloved was, otherwise
new cities and pâtés would bear her
name. But it's useless. Only velvet
growing under velvet, like a leaf hidden
safely in another leaf. Light in darkness.
Unending adagios. That's how tired freedom
breathes. Biographers argue only
over details. Why he tormented
his nephew Karl so much. Why
he walked so fast. Why he didn't go
to London. Apart from that, everything is clear.
We don't know what music is. Who speaks
in it. To whom it is addressed. Why it is
so obstinately silent. Why it circles and returns
instead of giving a straight answer
as the Gospel demands. Prophecies
were not fulfilled. The Chinese didn't reach
the Rhine. Once more, it turned out that
the real world doesn't exist, to the immense
relief of antiquaries. The secret was hidden
somewhere else, not in soldiers'
knapsacks, but in a few notebooks.
Grillparzer, he, Chopin. Generals are
cast in lead and in tinsel to
give hell's flame a moment of respite
after kilowatts of straw. Unending adagios,
but first and foremost joy, wild
joy of shape, the laughing sister of death.

Bill Holm

Heavenly Length

Schubert does go on, doesn't he?
Don't you find him a bit much?
How much wine is enough
to wash down the bread?
Is there water enough to cover
the barges under Lake Superior?
Does the sun put out too much light?
Are there enough words
in the dictionary yet?
Too many teeth in the whale's jaw?
How many beautiful women
are too many? Will the men find them?
How much Schubert is too much?
Is it far from your left ear
to the top of the Greenland ice?
How many breaths do you intend
to breathe before you die?
Do you want these questions answered?
Someone is singing a long song.
Careful! It's getting inside.

Lisel Mueller

ROMANTICS

JOHANNES BRAHMS AND CLARA SCHUMANN

The modern biographers worry
"how far it went," their tender friendship.
They wonder just what it means
when he writes he thinks of her constantly,
his guardian angel, beloved friend.
The modern biograpers ask
the rude, irrelevant question
of our age, as if the event
of two bodies meshing together
establishes the degree of love,
forgetting how softly Eros walked
in the nineteenth century, how a hand
held overlong or a gaze anchored
in someone's eyes could unseat a heart,
and nuances of address not known
in our egalitarian language
could make the redolent air
tremble and shimmer with the heat
of possibility. Each time I hear
the Intermezzi, sad
and lavish in their tenderness,
I imagine the two of them
sitting in a garden
among late-blooming roses
and dark cascades of leaves,
letting the landscape speak for them,
leaving us nothing to overhear.

Jan Zwicky

Brahms' Clarinet
Quintet in B Minor, Op. 115

That we shall not forget to honour
brown, its reedy clarities.

And, though the earth is dying
and the names of its diseases
spread from the fencelines, Latinate:
a bright field
ribboned with swath.

That the mind's light could be filtered
as: a porch, late afternoon,
a trellised rose,
                    which is to say
a truth in nostalgia:
if we steel ourselves against regret
we will not grow more graceful,
but less

That a letter might honestly
begin, *Dear beloved.*

Grace Schulman

FROM THE NEW WORLD

Orange alert has glared over this city
since terror acquired colors. Orange,
not yellow, not even yellow elevated.

Before Dvořăk's Ninth, at Lincoln Center,
guards worry my handbag, stuffed with war news.
Oak leaves stick to pavement, yellow-to-orange

and high orange, brightest before they wither.
This year they sadden us. Talk was of endings,
not leaves but unrecurrent lives, and yet

with others now, we sink into a hush
like sanderlings that fly on a soundless cue.
Once the composer said his symphony

was Czech, as he was, that he added
"From the New World" in the final draft,
an offering for three years in America,

but in an oboe's long, plaintive vibrato,
I hear the phrases of Hasidic melodies,
African chants, come-thou's and *kyries*

I caught once on a street corner downtown,
four blocks merging like a napkin's points.
I raced a traffic light's orange-to-red

to find a synagogue confronting churches,
Baptist and Roman, eyeing one another.
High above street whines, music soared in quarrels,

moans, blues, echoed laments, and hymns that wafted
together from stone. It took a Czech patriot
to restore that day. Now the people cheer

so loud you'd think a New World is beginning,
the clamor telling us this world will do
as long as we can have some more of it.

Outside, the fountain shoots the stars.
We glance upward, smiling, even when
a leaf spins down to concrete, crisp, high orange.

Frank O'Hara

On Rachmaninoff's Birthday

It is your 86th birthday
and I am sitting crying at the corner
of Ninth Street and Avenue A
one swallow doesn't make a summer
this coffee is terribly tepid

sometimes the 2nd Symphony sounds like Purcell
sometimes it sounds like *Wozzeck*'s last act

where is J. F. Donnelly and his Russian wolfhounds?
where is his wife, Helen? where is the cigar-smell
and the hootings in the studio while I practice?

a day of dismay is a day to remember
night doesn't come, and feeling dissipates

as the disgusting blackness of light
refuses to go off and leave melancholy
to nourish its roots of perversity
perhaps it will turn green like a potato

the ability to sing is ordinary
the ability to play is exceptional

where we can shroud ourselves in the
mechanized clarity of emotional vandalism we
do not see your owlish obstinacy staring back

Diane Ackerman

RACHMANINOFF'S PSYCHIATRIST

I'm listening to Rachmaninoff's
Piano Concerto No. 2,
which he dedicated to Dr. Dahl,
the psychiatrist who guided him
through the straits of fever,
not long after Sergei had heard
his own first symphony played.
Horrified by its many defects
which seemed a sewage of noise,
he had fled the hall, ashamed,
a quagmire of self-doubt.

We cannot know all the sounds
Dahl and he exchanged,
but rubbing one word against another,
Dahl gradually restored
Sergei's confidence. History tells
that Dahl used affirmations
and auto-suggestion:
"You will compose again."
"You will write a piano concerto."
"You will write with great facility."
Repeated until the words saturated
His gift from head to fingers.

In truth, nothing can kill a gift,
but it may become anemic
from great shock or stress—
a sprain of the emotions will do,
or a traffic accident of the heart,
or a failure dire as a clanging bell.

For two years, Dahl worked
on Sergei's shattered will.
At last he collected up his senses
in a burst of blood fury
and composed his triumphant
2nd Piano Concerto,
full of tenderness and yearning,
beguiling melodies, raging passion,
and long sensuous preludes
to explosive climaxes,
frenzy followed by strains
of mysticism and trance.

Loaded with starry melodies,
it was a map of his sensibility,
and a wilderness rarely known
—the intense life of an artist
seen in miniature, with rapture expressed
as all-embracing sound.

Will you tell me if you know,
how Dahl might have received
such a gift? I cannot imagine it.
With hugs and shared enthusiasm?
With an austere thank you?
In his private moments, did he weep
at the privilege allowed him?
For a time he held the exposed heart
of a great artist, cupped his hands
around it like a flame, blew gently,
patiently, until it flared again.

For that, he earned the blessings
of history, and soothed millions
of hungry souls he would never meet.
Listening to Rachmaninoff's
concerto today, intoxicated by its fever,
I want to kiss the hands of Dahl,
but he is beyond my touch or game.
Allow me to thank you in his name.

J. D. McClatchy

NIGHT PIECE

I remember an excursion I made with Ravel
from Clarens to Varese, near Lake Maggiore,
to buy Varese paper. The town was very crowded
and we could not find two hotel rooms or even
two beds, so we slept together in one.

—Igor Stravinsky

I. *Ravel's Insomnia*

Sylph of that cold ceiling, your papered sky
Runs with waterstains from whose stream
Two mouths will never drink the same theme.
In the window casing phrases liquefy.

The doused streetlamps, the branches budded, slick
With drizzled lacquers, a rafter spar—these blacks
Are merely notes that midnight's blurred attacks
Fumble for through backlit rhetoric,

The stave of shadows across the wall and floor.
But white's your music, a teacher said, the sheet
With no instructions, counterpane and pleat,
The fountain plume that spills into a score.

This dozing firebird beside me knows
What lies beneath a measure's candid look,
What chances went to waste when he mistook
The silence, even when his eyes were closed.

Now all's reversed. A hush. The notes will dance
Themselves to death, like raindrops on the tile.
Again the window's page is turned. A stile.
Meadow glare. My parents. This bright expanse.

II. *Stravinsky's Dream*

Islands floating south
Ice islands   blue flames
On a bowl of thick oil

Frost petals come to rest
On the watercrust
The river turns   loops

Scalloped clouds
The cherries open
Like fan blades

Springlight seams
Snowcapped needles
Edge the pineswitch

Inside   a moist inkstone
Her cheek bent to paper
The rice powder streaks

Two starlings in a field
On the sun's furrows
Whiter forms in flight

From winter's one question
All its darkened news
Folded in that paper

Music in Nature

Mary Oliver

SUCH SINGING IN THE WILD BRANCHES

It was spring
and finally I heard him
among the first leaves—
then I saw him clutching the limb

in an island of shade
with his red-brown feathers
all trim and neat for the new year.
First, I stood still

and thought of nothing.
Then I began to listen.
Then I was filled with gladness—
and that's when it happened,

when I seemed to float,
to be, myself, a wing or a tree—
and I began to understand
what the bird was saying,

and the sands in the glass
stopped
for a pure white moment
while gravity sprinkled upward

like rain, rising,
and in fact
it became difficult to tell just what it was that was singing—
it was the thrush for sure, but it seemed

not a single thrush, but himself, and all his brothers,
and also the trees around them,
as well as the gliding, long-tailed clouds
in the perfectly blue sky—all, all of them

were singing.
And, of course, yes, so it seemed,
so was I.
Such soft and solemn and perfect music doesn't last

for more than a few moments.
It's one of those magical places wise people
like to talk about.
One of the things they say about it, that is true,

is that, once you've been there,
you're there forever.
Listen, everyone has a chance.
Is it spring, is it morning?

Are there trees near you,
and does your own soul need comforting?
Quick, then—open the door and fly on your heavy feet; the song
may already be drifting away.

Seamus Heaney

SONG

A rowan like a lipsticked girl,
Between the by-road and the main road
Alder trees at a wet and dripping distance
Stand off among the rushes.

There are the mud-flowers of dialect
And the immortelles of perfect pitch
And that moment when the bird sings very close
To the music of what happens.

Anthony Hecht

AN ORPHIC CALLING

For Mihaly Csikszentmihalyi

The stream's *courante* runs on, a *force majeure*,
A Major rippling of the pure mind of Bach,
Tumult of muscled currents, formed in far
Reaches of edelweiss, cloud and alpenstock,

Now folding into each other, flexing, swirled
In cables of perdurable muscle-tones,
Hurrying through this densely noted world,
Small chambers, studio mikes, Concorde headphones,

And from deep turbulent rapids, roiled and spun,
They rise in watery cycles to those proud
And purifying heights where they'd begun
On Jungfrau cliffs of edelweiss and cloud,

Piled cumuli, that *fons et origo*
("Too lofty and original to rage")
Of the mind's limpid unimpeded flow
Where freedom and necessity converge

And meet in a fresh curriculum of love
(Minor in grief, major in happiness)
As interlocking melodies contrive
Small trysts and liaisons, briefly digress

But only to return to Interlaken
Altitudes of clear trebles, crystal basses,
Fine reconciliations and unbroken
Threadings of fern-edged flutes tumbling races.

An Orphic calling it is, one that invites
Responsories, a summons to lute-led
Nature, as morning's cinnabar east ignites
And the instinctive sunflower turns its head.

Chuang Tzu

THE BREATH OF NATURE

When great Nature sighs, we hear the winds
Which, noiseless in themselves,
Awaken voices from other beings,
Blowing on them.
From every opening
Loud voices sound. Have you not heard
This rush of tones?

There stands the overhanging wood
On the steep mountain:
Old trees with holes and cracks
Like snouts, maws, and ears,
Like beam-sockets, like goblets,
Groves in the wood, hollows full of water:
You hear mooing and roaring, whistling,
Shouts of command, grumblings,
Deep drones, sad flutes.
One call awakens another in dialogue.
Gentle winds sing timidly,
Strong ones blast on without restraint.
Then the wind dies down. The openings
Empty out their last sound.
Have you not observed how all then trembles and subsides?

Yu replied: I understand:
The music of the earth sings through a thousand holes.
The music of man is made on flutes and instruments.
What makes the music of heaven?

Master Ki said:

Something is blowing on a thousand different holes.

Some power stands behind all this and makes the sound die
   down.

What is this power?

(Translated by Thomas Merton)

William Jay Smith

ORPHEUS

Orpheus with music charms the birds
And animals, the fish, the falling waves,
The stars that might be starfish overhead,
And dragons in their oriental caves.
By men who suffer he is always heard,
And speaks of life, and death which darkness brings,
Of roads that wind like sorrow through the trees,
Of forests, and of hills like sleeping kings.

Let us prepare; the god of music comes.
He will have laurel, and a fountain playing,
Moon-men ready at the kettledrums,
Fire-tipped lances, moon-white horses neighing,
Earth awakening from her tragic sleep,
The cool, ecstatic earth. O hear, O hear.

Bashō

The temple bell stops—
but the sound keeps coming
out of the flowers.

It's late fall
I wonder how the man
next door lives.

(Translated by Robert Bly)

Christina Georgina Rossetti

SONNET

A host of things I take on trust: I take
  The nightingales on trust, for few and far
  Between those actual summer moments are
When I have heard what melody they make.
So chanced it once at Como on the Lake:
  But all things, then, waxed musical; each star
  Sang on its course, each breeze sang in its ear,
All harmonies sang to senses wide awake.
All things in tune, myself not out of tune,
  Those nightingales were nightingales indeed:
  Yet truly an owl had satisfied my need,
And wrought a rapture underneath that moon,
  Or simple sparrow chirping from a reed;
For June that night glowed like doubled June.

Vaskô Popa

THE BLACKBIRD'S SONG

I the blackbird
Among birds the black-cowled
Fold and unfold my wings

Perform the rites in my field
In my beak I transform
A dewdrop and a grain of earth into song

O battle tomorrow be fine
That is to say be just

O verdant Queen grass
Be victorious you alone

O victory make the Queen's servants rejoice
Who feed her with crimson milk

Make her star-servants rejoice also
Who clothe her in living silver

I sing
And I burn one feather from my left pinion
That my song may be accepted

(Translated by Anne Pennington)

Susan Wheeler

BENNY THE BEAVER

Benny's tail would only drum.
All day while fellow beavers drug

The tree limbs to the riverbank
Benny slapped his tail to bang

A beat on hollow logs,
Keen for external analogs

To the hums within his head.
Benny's folks despaired. *Hey*

Weisenheimer shape up or else
Else he chose and so was helped

Clean off to military camp.
Would it cure his cooking

Beat from manifesting in-
Appropriately? Some feat. If

Benny tried, it didn't show.
All day long, his tail did shake

And set up such a strapping quake
The slaving campers riled. Quod

They: Benny's antics are not fair!
We'd love to lolligag on air,

Drumming for sheer sound alone.
Camp authorities thought alike

And banished Benny from the dam.
Dizzy, mournful Benny, damned

To wander up the mountainside,
Thought himself worthless. So

At the top he fixed to plummet off
The tip. Above the treeline odd

Silence fell. His footfalls each were bombs.
When suddenly up from far below

A curdling yell that seemed to make
His name. *Benny!* Did he hallucinate?

The trappers are coming! Benny,
Set to! Wha't's needed's a bang,

A racket by you! And Benny complied.
With his tail he raised a cacophony

That sent the traders highing tail,
Their bejesus out. *Hail Benny the Beaver, to*

Him We Owe All! And indeed, they did.
The Benjamin School for Drumming

Draws the best of beavers to study
Drums. And Benny? He's dead.

Hayden Carruth

ALL THINGS

The music of October
is the wild geese in the night
that bring me to rediscover
about the citylight

how all things are a song
unmeaning but profound
and fundamental to the tongue
we speak here on the ground.

St. Harmonie, let me sing
the music of October
in my loquacious stammering
till all hell freezes over.

Thomas Hardy

THE DARKLING THRUSH

I leant upon a coppice gate
    When Frost was spectre-gray,
And Winter's dregs made desolate
    The weakening eye of day.
The tangled bine-stems scored the sky
    Like strings of broken lyres,
And all mankind that haunted nigh
    Had sought their household fires.

The land's sharp features seemed to be
    The Century's corpse outleant,
His crypt the cloudy canopy,
    The wind his death-lament.
The ancient pulse of germ and birth
    Was shrunken hard and dry,
And every spirit upon earth
    Seemed fervorless as I.

At once a voice arose among
    The bleak twigs overhead
In a full-hearted evensong
    Of joy illimited;
An aged thrush, frail, gaunt, and small
    In blast-beruffled plume,
Had chosen thus to fling his soul
    Upon the growing gloom.

So little cause for carolings
    Of such ecstatic sound
Was written on terrestrial things
    Afar or nigh around,
That I could think there trembled through
    His happy good-night air
Some blessed Hope, whereof he knew
    And I was unaware.

Opera

William Meredith

ABOUT OPERA

It's not the tunes, although as I get older
Arias are what I hum and whistle.
It's not the plots—they continue to bewilder
In the tongue I speak and in several that I wrestle.

An image of articulateness is what it is:
Isn't this how we've always longed to talk?
Words as they fall are monotone and bloodless
But they yearn to take the risk these noises take.

What dancing is to the slightly spastic way
Most of us teeter through our bodily life
Are these measured cries to the clumsy things we say,
In the heart's duresses, on the heart's behalf.

Wayne Koestenbaum

from ODE TO ANNA MOFFO

What possesses me,
a maenad, is her first entrance,
when only the boy reading the liner notes
    absolutely knows
it is Anna Moffo and not
an impostor about to open her mouth
    and derange the air
    with a tone
introspective as a plant
alone with thoughts of her stem and her photosynthesis.

    On loose-leaf paper
I wrote down the names of the stars.
My roster still sleeps in the *Butterfly* case,
    as if *dramatis*
personae were frozen there
like Easter Island idols, punished, alert,
    exiled in a box
    whose fragrance,
when I open it, is dust
mingled with narcissus, scent of what I will never have:

    presence of her voice
    in the house
alive, so I may applaud,
while wind from a special effects machine streams through her
   hair.

Yves Bonnefoy

TO THE VOICE OF KATHLEEN FERRIER

All softness and irony assembled
For a farewell of crystal and haze.
The deep thrusts of the sword were near-silent,
The light of the blade was obscured.

I praise this voice mingled with gray,
Wavering in the distance of the song which died away
As if beyond pure forms there trembled
Another song, alone and absolute.

O light and light's nothingness, O you tears
Smiling higher than anguish or hope,
O swan, real place in unreal dark waters,
O wellspring in the very deep of evening!

It seems you know well the two shores:
The deepest sorrow and the highest joy.
Over there, in the light among the gray reeds
It seems that you draw from eternity.

(Translated by Anthony Rudolf)

James Wright

Poem for Kathleen Ferrier

1
I leaned to hear your song,
The breathing and the echo;
And when it dropped away,
I thought, for one deaf moment,
That I could never listen
To any other voice.

2
But the land is deep in sound.
The sleepy hares and crickets
Remember how to cry.
The birds have not forgotten
(The tanager, the sparrow)
the tumbled, rising tone.

3
The sounds go on, and on,
In spite of what the morning
Or evening dark has done.
We have no holy voices
Like yours to lift above us,
Yet we cannot be still.

4
All earth is loud enough.
Then why should I be sorry
(The owl scritches alive)
To stand before a shadow,
And see a cold piano
Half hidden by a drape?

5
No reason I can give.
Uttering tongues are busy,
Mount the diminished air
(The breathing and the echo)
Enough to keep the ear
Half satisfied forever.

J. D. McClatchy

CALLAS

Her voice: steeped in a rancid syrupy phlegm:
Whatever's not believed remains a grace
While again she invokes the power that yields:
Splintered timber and quick consuming flame:
The simplest way to take hold of the heart's
Complications, its pool of spilt religion:
A long black hair sweat-stuck to the skin:
The bitter sleep of the dying: the Jew in Berlin:
Who sent you here? the sharp blade pleads:
Stormcloud: thornhedge: starchill:
Blood bubble floating to the top of the glass:
The light, from fleshrise to soulset:
The world dragging the slow weight of its shame
Like the train of pomp: guttering candle: her voice.

Charles Gullans

On a Recording by Maria Cebotari

I hear your voice through these defective grooves.
Each revolution of the track removes
Something of your magnificence, your skill.
Each note, each time becomes more distant still.
So life's attrition, faster than it should,
Destroys your legacy, the fragile good
Of this recording through which you survive.
And I, who never heard you when alive,
Think of your final role, Eurydice—
Music will not assuage its irony—
And of the sad inhabitants of death,
Who are and who are not, Song without breath,
Distant magnificence that slowly fades
Into the emptiness of those mute shades.

Wislawa Szymborska

AGING OPERA SINGER

"Today he sings this way: tralala tra la.
But I sang it like this: tralala tra la.
Do you hear the difference?
And instead of standing here, he stands here
And looks this way, not this way,
Although she comes flying in from over there,
not over there, and not like today rampa pampa pam,
but quite simply rampa pampa pam,
the unforgettable Tschubek-Bombonieri,
only
who remembers her now—"

William Matthews

VA, PENSIERO

When Verdi lay dying, the Milanese
scattered straw for blocks around his house
to muffle the clatter of horses
so the Maestro could easily release

his breath, *piano*, no more fuss than that.
Someone reading across the room looked up:
the silence had gone slack. Soon enough,
as I thought when my father was first dead,

the consolations will begin. Time now
to spurn all balms, to hold up like a glass
of wine (*Libiamo!*) the malice
I hoarded, the blessings I held in my mouth

like spit, the spite I burnt for fuel.
Who snarls across the stage with a drawn sword;
who gives and then defiles his or her word,
unless it's me, or you? And we can't use

ever the hoard we didn't spend.
Now consolation means something.
And so three massed choirs poise to sing
Va, pensiero in February 1901.

Their visible, blobbed breath rose like a ghost
above the flower-barnacled coffin.
Fly, thought, the hymn begins, and like a falcon
thought goes, and like a falcon thought comes home.

Charles Tomlinson

A Night at the Opera

When the old servant reveals she is the mother
  Of the young count whose elder brother
Has betrayed him, the heroine, disguised
  As the Duke's own equerry, sings *Or'*
Che sono, pale from the wound she has received
  In the first act. The entire court
Realize what has in fact occurred and wordlessly
  The waltz song is to be heard now
In the full orchestra. And we, too,
  Recall that meeting of Marietta with the count
Outside the cloister in Toledo. She faints:
  Her doublet being undone, they find
She still has on the hair-shirt
  Worn ever since she was a nun
In Spain. So her secret is plainly out
  And Boccaleone (blind valet
To the Duke) confesses it is he (*Or' son'io*)
  Who overheard the plot to kidnap the dead
Count Bellafonte, to burn by night
  The high camp of the gipsy king
Alfiero, and by this stratagem quite prevent
  The union of both pairs of lovers.
Now the whole cast packs the stage
  Raging in chorus round the quartet—led
By Alfiero (having shed his late disguise)
  And Boccaleone (shock has restored his eyes):
Marietta, at the first note from the count
  (Long thought dead, but finally revealed
As Alfiero), rouses herself, her life
  Hanging by a thread of song, and the Duke,

Descending from his carriage to join in,
  Dispenses pardon, punishment and marriage.
Exeunt to the Grand March, Marietta
  (Though feebly) marching, too, for this
Is the "Paris" version where we miss
  The ultimate dénouement when at the command
Of the heroine (*Pura non son'*) Bellafonte marries
  The daughter of the gipsy king and

Kenneth Koch

At the Opera

Ah do you remember
                    the voice of Gianni Poggi
                                        in Firenze
"in tuo splendor'"
                    the clear light
                                        and easy division
of the Italian language
                    "aurora" so it sounds like
                                        Bobby Burns
it's another sign
                    Katherine is two—
                                        not quite—grand opera
and you still alive
                    "lucevan le stelle"
                                        and Gozzanno
in the morning
                    the true pink light
                                        and Gatto, the cat
who walked to our doorstep
                    from higher
                                        on the hill
I think, that led
                    someplace (Fiesole?)—
                                        "led" che splendore, "led"
and we, we were
                    led
                    Gianni Poggi was led
he was leading
                    but not the orchestra
                                        led

to his death

        alla sua morte

              che orror'

but not

      a real one

          he

was still alive

        when we left

            the theatre and came home.

Amy Lowell

AN OPERA HOUSE

Within the gold square of the proscenium arch,
A curtain of orange velvet hangs in stiff folds,
Its tassels jarring slightly when someone crosses the stage
  behind.
Gold carving edges the balconies,
Rims the boxes,
Runs up and down fluted pillars.
Little knife-stabs of gold
Shine out whenever a box door is opened.
Gold clusters
Flash in soft explosions
On the blue darkness,
Suck back to a point,
And disappear.
Hoops of gold
Circle necks, wrists, fingers,
Pierce ears,
Poise on heads
And fly up above them in coloured sparkles.
Gold!
Gold!
The opera house is a treasure-box of gold.
Gold in a broad smear across the orchestra pit:
Gold of horns, trumpets, tubas;
Gold—spun-gold, twittering-gold, snapping-gold
Of harps.
The conductor raises his baton,
The brass blares out
Crass, crude,
Parvenu, fat, powerful,

Golden.
Rich as the fat, clapping hands in the boxes.
Cymbals, gigantic, coin-shaped,
Crash.
The orange curtain parts
And the prima-donna steps forward.
One note,
A drop: transparent, iridescent,
A gold bubble,
It floats . . . floats . . .
And bursts against the lips of a bank president
In the grand tier.

Charles Gullans

ROSENKAVALIER

What does the mirror show you, Marschallin?
The past retreating at the speed of light,
The future raging to achieve the night,
The void from which Oktavian will lean
To give the kisses you had both forseen?

It is the pool in which your glories fall
And all your joys descend: the silver rose
In the silvering beauty of your brow still glows
A moment, but will vanish with the tall
And cruel brilliance of a waterfall.

Louise Glück

ORFEO

"J'ai perdu mon Eurydice. . . . "

I have lost my Eurydice,
I have lost my lover,
and suddenly I am speaking French
and it seems to me I have never been in better voice;
it seems these songs
are songs of a high order.

And it seems one is somehow expected to apologize
for being an artist,
as though it were not entirely human to notice these fine points.
And who knows, perhaps the gods never spoke to me in Dis,
never singled me out,
perhaps it was all illusion.

O Eurydice, you who married me for my singing,
why do you turn on me, wanting human comfort?
Who knows what you'll tell the furies
when you see them again.

Tell them I have lost my beloved;
I am completely alone now.
Tell them there is no music like this
without real grief.

In Dis, I sang to them; they will remember me.

James Merrill

ORFEO

Ah downward through the dark coulisse,
Impelled to walk the stage of hell,
Unwind as in a theater gilt and puce
His opulence of pain until

Each damned soul dropped its trembling fan
(Which in the gusts of wooing trembled still)
And wept to hear him: it was then
Sickeningly he divined, but with an odd thrill,

Among the shadows of a box
That brow, that hand outspread upon
The plush worn bare, a white peacock's
Genius at dusk on a dissolving lawn,

Her loss within his music's rise and fall
Having become perpetual.

John Smith

Death at the Opera

Is this what death is like? I sit
Dressed elegantly in black and white, in an expensive seat,
Watching Violetta expire in Covent Garden.
How beautiful she is. As her voice lures me toward her death
The strings of the orchestra moisten my eyes with tears,
Though the tenor is too loud. Is this what death is like?
No one moves. Violetta coughs; stumbles toward the bed.
Twenty miles away in the country my father is dying.
Violetta catches at her throat. Let me repeat: my father
Is dying in a semi-detached house on a main road
Twenty miles off in the country. The skull is visible.

I do not want it to end. How exquisitely moving is death,
The approach to it. The lovers sob. Soon they will be wrenched
    apart.
How romantic it all is. Her hand is a white moth
Fluttering against the coverlet of the bed. The bones
Of my father's hands poke through his dry skin.
His eyes look into a vacancy of space. He spits into a cup.
In a few moments now Violetta will give up the ghost;
The doctor, the maid, the tenor who does not love her, will sob.
Almost, our hearts will stop beating. How refreshed we have
    been.
My father's clothes, too large for his shrunken frame,
Made him look like a parcel. Ah! The plush curtains are opening.

The applause! The applause! It drowns out the ugly noise
Of my father's choking and spitting. The bright lights
Glitter far more than the hundred watt bulb at home.
Dear Violetta! How she enjoys the flowers, like wreaths,
Showered for her own death. She gathers them to her.
We have avoided the coffin. I think that my father
Would like a box of good plain beech, being a man
From Buckinghamshire, a man of the country, a man of the soil.
I have seen my father, who is fond of animals, kill a cat
That was old and in pain with a blow from the edge of his palm.
He buried it in the garden, but I cannot remember its name.

Now the watchers are dispersing; the taxis drive away
Black in the black night. A huddle of people wait
Like mourners round the stage door. Is this what death is like?
For Violetta died after all. It is merely a ghost,
The voice gone, the beautiful dress removed, who steps in the
    rain.
Art, I conceive, is not so removed from life; for we look at death
Whether real or imagined, from an impossible distance
And somewhere a final curtain is always descending.
The critics are already phoning their obituaries to the papers.
I do not think God is concerned with such trivial matters
But, father, though there will be no applause, die well.

Howard Nemerov

The End of the Opera

To Mona Van Duyn

Knowing that what he witnessed was only art,
He never wept while the show was going on.

But the curtain call could always make him cry.
When the cast came forward hand in hand
Bowing and smiling to the clatter of applause,
Tired, disheveled, sweating through the paint,
Radiant with our happiness and theirs,
Illuminati of the spot and flood,
Yet much the same as ordinary us.

The diva, the soubrette, the raisonneur,
The inadequate hero, the villain, his buffoon,
All equalled in the great reality
And living proof that life would follow life . . .

Though back of that display there'd always be,
He knew, money and envy, the career,
Tomorrow and tomorrow—it didn't seem
At that moment as if it mattered much
Compared with their happiness and ours
As we wept about the role, about the real,
And how their dissonances harmonized
As we applauded us: *ite, missa est.*

Richard Howard

Richard Wagner
A DISPUTED PORTRAIT BY NADAR JEUNE

No props—for once we have you unstaged, ideal
      genius at forty without
wadded-silk dressing-gown, wine-velvet beret,

      a villa filled with idols.
You stare off-camera at—what? Here at least
      there is more than meets the ear

cocked, this moment, for Frau Wesendonck's praises
      and for Cosima's prayers—
so much more ardent, at sixteen, than Minna's:

      a few infidelities
will bring far less sorrow than the long-drawn-out
      disloyalty of desire.

What we see is what we dream you must have been,
      boldly readying yourself
for what Baudelaire called the greatest honor

      a poet can have: to do
no more and no less than what he intended.
      Until your will had been done,

the difference between sanity and hysteria,
      illusion and reality,
had always been a matter of time: what was

real, what was sane, had always
lasted longer—only truth was continuous.
        You would alter that, transform

our fears and even our fatigue, you would force
        time to change shape and by cold
legerdemain, from Ortrud to Klingsor, make

        event, mere happening, into
duration, having discovered the center
        of our every appetite

is in its metamorphoses. Wait, though—dates
        conflict, the size of the plate
is wrong, and you hated Nadar; for a man

        just over five feet, could these
long shanks be yours? Experts shrug, and we are left
        with the old dissatisfactions:

complete understanding of a dream includes
        the knowledge that it is one,
and such knowledge wakes us up. This is not you.

Jazz & Blues

Sandra McPherson

The Ability to Make a Face Like a Spider While Singing Blues: Junior Wells

Who knows if they sing in their web
or while hunting—they may never have tried
their voices, and what is a spider throat?
But until we know that, a singer thinking
about a *mean black spider* becomes one
without thinking and intends to race
the winged one through the stickiest place.
Cock your head; when you squint, the
light will throw you reasonable prey,
what you deserve, a gleam, a solo look,
a song to repair the break of day.

Mark Doty

Almost Blue
CHET BAKER, 1921–1988

If Hart Crane played trumpet
he'd sound like you, your horn's dark city

miraculous and broken over and over,
scale-shimmered, every harbor-flung hour

and salt-span of cabled longing,
every waterfront, the night-lovers' rendezvous.

This is the entrance
to the city of you, sleep's hellgate,

and two weeks before the casual relinquishment
of your hold—light needling

on the canal's gleaming haze
and the buds blaring like horns—

two weeks before the end, Chet,
and you're playing like anything,

singing *stay little valentine*
stay

and taking so long there are worlds sinking
between the notes, this exhalation

no longer a voice but a rush of air,
brutal, from the tunnels under the river,

the barges' late whistles you only hear
when the traffic's stilled

by snow, a city hushed and
distilled into one rush of breath,

yours, into the microphone
and the ear of that girl

in the leopard-print scarf,
one long kiss begun on the highway

and carried on dangerously,
the Thunderbird veering

on the coast road: glamor
of a perfectly splayed fender,

dazzling lipstick, a little pearl of junk,
some stretch of road breathless

and traveled into . . . Whoever she is
she's the other coast of you,

and just beyond the bridge the city's
long amalgam of ardor and indifference

is lit like a votive
then blown out. Too many rooms unrented

in this residential hotel,
and you don't want to know

why they're making that noise in the hall;
you're going to wake up in any one of the

how many ten thousand
locations of trouble and longing

going out of business forever everything must go
wake up and start wanting.

It's so much better when you don't want:
nothing falls then, nothing lost

but sleep and who wanted that
in the pearl this suspended world is,

in the warm suspension and glaze
of this song everything stays up

almost forever in the long
glide sung into the vein,

one note held almost impossibly
almost blue and the lyric takes so long

to open, a little blood
blooming: *there's no love song   finer*

but how strange the change
from major to minor

everytime
we say goodbye

and you leaning into that warm
haze from the window, Amsterdam,

late afternoon glimmer
a blur of buds

breathing in the lindens
and you let go and why not

Hayden Carruth

BILLIE HOLIDAY

Here lies a lady. Day was her double pain,
Pride and compassion equally gone wrong.
At night she sang, "Do you conceive my song?"
And answered in her torn voice, "Don't explain."

Yusef Komunyakaa

TENEBRAE

May your spirit sleep in peace
One grain of corn can fill the silo.
        —The Samba of Tanzania

In memory of Richard Johnson

You try to beat loneliness
out of a drum,
but cries only spring
from your mouth.
Synapse & memory—
the day quivers like dancers
with bells on their feet,
weaving a path of songs
to bring you back,
to heal our future
with the old voices
we breathe. Sometimes
our hands hang like weights
anchoring us inside
ourselves. You can go
to Africa on a note
transfigured into a tribe
of silhouettes in a field
of reeds, & circling the Cape
of Good Hope you find
yourself in Paris
backing The Hot Five.

You try to beat loneliness
out of a drum.
As you ascend
the crescendo,
please help us touch what remains
most human. Your absence
brings us one step closer
to the whole cloth
& full measure.
We're under the orange trees again, as you work life
back into the double-headed
drumskin with a spasm
of fingertips
till a chant leaps
into the dreamer's mouth.

You try to beat loneliness
out of a drum, always
coming back to opera & baseball.
A constellation of blood-tuned
notes shake against the night
forest bowed to the ground
by snow & ice. Yes,
this kind of solitude
can lift you up
between two thieves.

You can do a drumroll
that rattles slavechains
on the sea floor.

What wrong makes you
loop that silent knot
& step up on the gallows-
chair? What reminds you of the wounded paradise
we stumbled out of?

You try to beat loneliness
out of a drum,
searching for a note
of kindness here at the edge
of this grab-wheel,
with little or no dragline
beyond the flowering trees
where only ghosts live—
no grip to clutch the truth
under a facade of skylarks.

Nicholas Christopher

JAZZ

When my mother was pregnant with me
she worked at a record company
that produced jazz
(jive jump swing & bebop)
and spent many afternoons
that summer and fall
at recording sessions
on the West Side of Manhattan
talking with the musicians between takes
sipping Coca-Cola
eating sandwiches with the engineers
closing her eyes
and tapping her feet to the music
and me there inside her
drums bass piano trumpet & trombone
and all those saxophones
working on my sensibilities
such as they were
like someone at the bottom of a swimming pool
who hears a band playing up above
under the moon on a warm night
taking it in
under the bigger bass of her heartbeat
all those rhythms
and crosscurrents of sound
(and moving to it?)
all those rhythms
I must have been listening for
months later when I was born
my ear cocked for them

in the loud world
and where were they?
all those rhythms

Jennifer Grotz

JAZZ IN PARIS

is a wet blue street, an American name
cartoonish in a Parisian arrondissement,
    a dance floor packed with chairs
where I slip into some form of listening
    that requires almost no movement and
looking around I see women
    leaning toward, in the arms of
men smoking cigarettes in tight leather jackets.

The musicians speak to the crowd
in English, making my accent lazy
    when the waiter comes around.
If I don't pour the beer in a glass I may be thrown out
    for behaving *"provocateur."* I want to be
back in New Orleans, stamping cigarettes out
    on the dark wood floor of Tipitina's
under fans that don't do the job once the people arrive,
    I want to be down by Armstrong Park,
where the best stuff is: Joe's Cozy Corner, Russell's Cool Spot,
    the Little People's Place with free red beans and
seats on barrels in a dark room riddled with bent knees
    and trumpets aimed at ceilings
(not the *"oui, oui"* of the waiter).

My body slouches and two fingers dreamily
cradle a cigarette, knowing what it means to miss . . .
    all that brass gleaming under red lights,
making you feel rich. Serious French cool cats
    slurp appreciations: *"C'est hip, non?*
C'est happening!" Fingers snapping.

When I first heard Nina Simone's
"Ne Me Quitte Pas," I heard it sung by a man at his most
   pathetic:
      Laisse-moi devenir l'ombre de ton ombre . . .
I subscribed to this pleading long ago and so
      —let me become the shadow of your shadow—
the drunk Frenchman lying across the table
      hamming up "Ne Me Quitte Pas" didn't startle me.
The olive garnishes he sent rolling off the tablecloth
      and across the floor didn't startle me.
What did: my private desires broadcast through horns,
      gleaming in gin glasses across the room.

Kevin Young

SATCHMO

SIDE A—
the face handled
careful, black

wax grooves
going round
in an endless

endless grin—
King Louie
Armstrong

blowing like no
tomorrow
Oooh hoo

*I wanna be
like you-who*—
Pops wipes his brow

with a kerchief
as if cleaning
a needle, a skipping

dusty L.P.
*An ape like me
would love to be*

human too.

SIDE B—
his bull

horn muffled,
sounding fog—
labels spun

too fast
to read. Heebie
Jeebies. *Is*

you is or is
you ain't—
Satchelmouth

Old Scratch,
between the devil
& the deep

blue sea—his Hot Fives
scat, out-play
Beezlebub on a good

day—two horns
twisted
up out his hair—

Terrance Hayes

"Boogie Woogie Blues"

Year of Release: 1948
Running Time: 10 minutes
Cast: vocalist and pianist Hadda Brooks performing three songs

If you have slept in a house made of nothing but a smile
That drooped around your neck like a five pound chain;
If you have whittled all the virtuous words in the Bible down

To *Amen* the way pillow talk can be whittled down to a tongue,
You know the name of my song: "Don't Take Your Love from Me."

Don't take your love away from me. Your house key.
Your toothbrush. Your swing and sweet scripture
Of touching and preacher's breath. Don't take your fingertips

And hunger from my ears. I know the lyrics
Of the oldest love song: "Don't You Think I Ought to Know."

Don't you think I ought to know, Baby, the doctrine of the Blues,
The spells and fevers of the Blues, the Blues' epistemologies?
I know the lyrics of the oldest love songs. And the new ones too.

Why bother rise and dress now that you are gone?
Why bother boogie woogie? "I'm Tired of Everything but You."

Grace Schulman

BLUE IN GREEN

Blue in green: baywater seen through grasses
that quiver over it, stirring the air,
slanted against the water's one-em dashes.
Each blade is a brushstroke on thin rice paper,

unrehearsed, undrafted, no revision,
right on the first take. In "Blue in Green,"
on tenor sax, John Coltrane fills the blues
with mournful chords on scales older than Jubal's,

ending in air. He'd not played it before
that recording, with that piano and bass
rising alone and, birds in flight, together.
Right on the first take. Improvisation,

he called it, but it must have been foreseen,
like the painter's brushstroke. A wrong line
could blot the composition, snag the paper.
It had to be unstudied, like a tern's cry,

and natural, like a rope's clink on a mast
with wind as bass player, huge and invisible.
If only I could remember the past
without regret for the windrose petal's fall,

for words unspoken, and without remorse
for loves withheld. Rough-draft mistakes.
If only my heart could teach my hands
to play, and get it right on the first take.

Gabrielle Calvocoressi

A LOVE SUPREME

You beautiful, broke-
back horse of my heart.   Proud,
debonair, not quite there

in the head.   You current
with no river in sight.
Current as confetti

after parades.   You
small-town.   Italian
ice shop next to brothels

beside the highway.
Sweet and sweaty. You high
as a kite coming

down.   You suburban sprawled
on the bed.   You dead?   Not
nearly.   Not yet.

Bruce Bond

THELONIOUS SPHERE MONK

Take any solo session from the Riverside
years, those long trapped breaths of dissonance
like smoke, a holding back of fulfillment
that becomes just that, our glad and broken
contract, and you hear the great sad boulders

of chords thump into place, foundation stones
for later work, entire soaring tenements
of work. Difficult at times, the way he kept
everyone waiting, those hours he stumbled
through uncharted tunes, tape rolling, until

his stagger had a heart's precision to it,
a largesse of hands startled by choice.
Which is why, beyond the scarred edifice
of tone clusters and uneven strides, each room's
waste of cups and ashes, beyond the nights

his strings soured in a New York basement,
there's a lightness here, a compulsion
to surprise. Less an end to silence
than a yielding to its wants, to the bloom
of poverty and water inside it:

sound as the hard fruit of deprivation.
And though you see him stab at the odd key,
his finger blunted like a cigarette,
it's not rage at a world slow to forgive
or understand, not merely; not the chronic

deafness of taxis and jail clerks, the phony
drug charge that left him jobless; but more
a private joy working on its problem.
To raze and resurrect, to resurrect by razing.
There are moments he seems so thickly bound

in the black suns of his eyes, his face
bearded as a buffalo, mumbling in the shade
of a dark-felt hat. How better to inhabit
the pride of disappointment, to spark
against the corners, making a language

out of failure to speak—though in time
failure became just that, a handful of days
he refused it all: the phone calls, his wife,
his health, his music. They block-and-tackled
his spinet through the high window of a cramped

apartment. Who was he to suffer fools,
let alone his own hands; and it came on
so swiftly: the thinning of his face
in the stream of silence. Soon his piano
too was a black chest of wire and dust.

And memory was small comfort. All his life
the giant spools of pleasure and tape flowed
in one direction: how he lived, he died,
the high gothic cathedral of his style
eroding, its stones condemned, windows boarded.

Michael S. Harper

FOR BUD

For Bud Powell

Could it be, Bud
that in slow galvanized
fingers beauty seeped
into *bop* like Bird
weed and Diz clowned—
Sugar waltzing
back into dynamite,
sweetest left hook you
ever dug, baby;
could it violate violence
Bud, like Leadbelly's
chaingang chuckle,
the candied yam
twelve string clutch
of all blues:
there's no rain
anywhere, soft
enough for you.

Harvey Shapiro

How Charlie Shavers Died

He had a gig
but he was hurting.
His doctor said, play the date,
then check into the hospital.
That night, when the party ended
and the band packed up,
Charlie started to give stuff away—
his watch, his rings—to the women
in the room. Then
he circled the room with his horn
playing: "For all I know we may never meet again."
At this point, the man who was telling the story
in the locker room at the Manhattan Plaza gym
and who had sung the line slowly, with
a pause between each word, began to cry.

Jan Zwicky

BILL EVANS: *ALONE*

Sound that makes night fall around it
like the glow from a reading lamp.

Rain on the roof, straight down.
The name of your name
spoken without another's.

Rubato is a hand
you thought indifferent
laid, briefest of moments,
on your sleeve.

It walks away, then,
that sound, without looking back.
Lights up a Lucky. Says

we hadn't the ghost of a chance, says never
let me go.

David Lehman

RADIO

I left it
on when I
left the house
for the pleasure
of coming back
ten hours later
to the greatness
of Teddy Wilson
After You've Gone
on the piano
in the corner
of the bedroom
as I enter
in the dark

Paul Blackburn

LISTENING TO SONNY ROLLINS
AT THE FIVE SPOT

There will be many other nights like
be standing here with someone, some
one
someone
some-one
some
some
some
some
some
some
one
there will be other songs
a-nother fall, another—spring, but
there will never be a-noth, noth
anoth
noth
anoth-er
noth-er
noth-er
      Other lips that I may kiss,
but they won't thrill me like
         thrill me like
            like yours
used to
      dream a million dreams

but how can they come
when there
            never be
a-noth—

Billy Collins

Nightclub

You are so beautiful and I am a fool
to be in love with you
is a theme that keeps coming up
in songs and poems.
There seems to be no room for variation.
I have never heard anyone sing
I am so beautiful
and you are a fool to be in love with me,
even though this notion has surely
crossed the minds of women and men alike.
You are so beautiful, too bad you are a fool
is another one you don't hear.
Or, you are a fool to consider me beautiful.
That one you will never hear, guaranteed.

For no particular reason this afternoon
I am listening to Johnny Hartman
whose dark voice can curl around
the concepts of love, beauty, and foolishness
like no one else's can.
It feels like smoke curling up from a cigarette
someone left burning on a baby grand piano
around three o'clock in the morning;
smoke that billows up into the bright lights
while out there in the darkness
some of the beautiful fools have gathered
around little tables to listen,
some with their eyes closed,
others leaning forward into the music

as if it were holding them up,
or twirling the loose ice in a glass,
slipping by degrees into a rhythmic dream.
Yes, there is all this foolish beauty,
borne beyond midnight,
that has no desire to go home,
especially now when everyone in the room
is watching the large man with the tenor sax
that hangs from his neck like a golden fish.
He moves forward to the edge of the stage
and hands the instrument down to me
and nods that I should play.
So I put the mouthpiece to my lips
and blow into it with all my living breath.
We are all so foolish,
my long bebop solo begins by saying,
so damn foolish
we have become beautiful without even knowing it.

Jack Kerouac

Bird was gone
    and distance grew
Immensely white

Performances

Jane Flanders

THE HANDBELL CHOIR

Twelve children, twelve gray geese in starched
collars, file onstage. Like their bells,
which are set out buffet-style on a long table,
they are graduated. The gym, with its folding chairs
and stale air, seems wrong;
they belong in a cloister or small pond.

The director, also in gray, appears.
They will play "Geese . . . " no, "Sheep May Safely Graze,"
in honor of Bach's three hundredth birthday.
Her raised hand, their rapt stance quiet us,
who suddenly seem to be listening
for a rush of wings. But the advent
is simply that of a sweet chord.

With a flick of the wrist, each bell is rung
then silenced on the breast. No hurry.
They take all the repeats,
arms rising and falling stiffly, like clockwork
hammers sounding over the roofs of Eisenach
on a March day for the baptism of the infant
Johann Sebastian. We think of sheep and lambs
in spitting snow. The church is clammy, water cold
on a baby's head, he cries a bit—
another miraculous, ordinary birth.

Having happened, the past is safe.
This is the dangerous moment, the melody passed
from hand to hand. Tirelessly, ancient-eyed,
they raise their bells as if in blessing, yes,
someone here, now, is blessing us.

Mary Stewart Hammond

SEEING MOZART'S PIANO QUARTET IN E-FLAT MAJOR IN THE OLD WHALING CHURCH, EDGARTOWN

They wait, five women in black,
before a wall painted such a flat, soft gray
it reads as silence, or sky.
The pianist's hands curve over the keyboard.
The page turner leans toward the pianist's score.
The violinist, the violist, the cellist
bring their bows near the strings.   Fluted pilasters
rise into an arch ceiling high, framing them.
The church, classic Greek Revival
straight from the style books, and *retarditaire* at that,
is 57 years younger than the music you are about
not to hear, but with its pillars, its two
center aisles dividing the nave into three parts,
in its classicism and its purity, it is useful
for showing the architecture of this sonata.
The thing about music, it takes place in time,
and can't be seen.   Nor can it be heard in a poem.

A colorless, unfinished, 8 o'clock sky pauses
in triple hung windows flanking the pilasters.
Scrub oak darken the lower panes.
The pianist nods.   We know by the musicians'
movements that Mozart's allegro begins its lift
up off the pages on the music stands, but on this page
there are only the visuals.   The music is silent
as a black and white picture show
before the arrival of sound. The pianist misses

some notes. The violist looks at the violinist,
her hair a stubble three months after chemo.
Strings shine on the black necks of the instruments.
The musicians' fingers climb up and down like spiders,
thumbs hugging the backsides of the necks.
They glide their bows, or make them tiptoe,
forearms rigid, across the strings.

The second theme's leading motif, almost lost
under the angelic, repeats and repeats
like supplications. It is one of Mozart's miracles,
this longing under joy, the flirtations with death
balancing lyricism, but you have only my word for it.
The ensemble coaxes the allegretto
and transubstantiation from wooden boxes. In a year
the violist will be dead. The music breathes
in the musicians' bodies. You can see it
in their shoulders, their spines, their wrists, their fingers,
and the white grid of the windows' muntins cages the black sky.
Even where the bottom sashes open to the summer air,
the night is held back until the musicians stop,
hold their poses, wait, five seconds, twelve,
for the last notes to find home and fling up their arms
pumped with arrival. They rise, bowing
before the sky of the soft gray wall,
leaving us in our humanness under the electric lights.

Wayne Koestenbaum

from ODE TO ANNA MOFFO

My debut is dark—
a kindergarten cameo
appearance playing imported tambourine.
    I stood on the stage
and rattled a white disk, waiting
for the curtain to drape my futility.
        Reward for ceaseless
        and timely
performance was candy corn.
I bit the black stripe off the triangle and saved the heart

    of the confection
an orange, blunt pyramid—for a day
when I could comprehend its antecedents.
    We learned to read notes
by a perverse pedagogy;
semibreves hovered outside the pale of clef
        or staff, and we guessed
        pitch by faith,
deprived of system. I gripped,
with the will of a colonialist, my tambourine,

        as if it were sky
        stirred, jangled,
and abandoned by a boy's hand,
as if the sky depended on a boy to make it sound.

Howard Nemerov

LINES & CIRCULARITIES
ON HEARING CASALS' RECORDING OF THE SIXTH SUITE

Deep in a time that cannot come again
Bach thought it through, this lonely and immense
Reflexion wherein our sorrows learn to dance.
And deep in the time that cannot come again
Casals recorded it. Playing it back,
And bending now over the instrument,
I watch the circling stillness of the disc,
The tracking inward of the tone-arm, enact
A mystery wherein the music shares:
How time, that comes and goes and vanishes
Never to come again, can come again.

How many silly miracles there are
That will not save us, neither will they save
The world, and yet they are miraculous;
The tone-arm following the spiral path
While moving inward on a shallow arc,
Making the music that companions it
Through winding ways to silence at the close;
The delicate needle that navigates these canyons
By contact with the edges, not the floor;
Black plastic that has memorized and kept
In its small striations whatever it was told
By the master's mind and hand and bow and box,
Making such definite shudderings in the air
That Bach's intent arises from the tomb . . .
The Earth, that spins around upon herself

In the simple composition of Light and Dark,
And varying her distance on the Sun
Makes up the Seasons and the Years, and Time
Itself, whereof the angels make record;
The Sun, swinging his several satellites
Around himself and slowly round the vast
Galactic rim and out to the unknown
Past Vega at the apex of his path;
And all this in the inward of the mind,
Where the great cantor sings his songs to God . . .

The music dances to its inner edge
And stops. The tone-arm lifts and cocks its head
An instant, as if listening for something
That is no longer there but might be; then
Returns to rest, as with a definite click
The whole strange business turns itself off.

Jan Zwicky

MUSICIANS

I pass a bunch of musicians in the street.
It's about 12:30, rehearsal just over, they're
standing around outside the side door of the church.
A good rehearsal: and it's April. They're laughing,
horsing around, talking about shoes, or taxes, where
to go for lunch, anything
except what their heads are full of.
It's a kind of helplessness, you can see
they're still breathing almost in unison, like people
the searchlight has passed over
and spared, their attention
lifts, swerves, settles; even
the gravel dust stuttering at their feet
is coherent.

Wendell Berry

A MUSIC

I employ the blind mandolin player
in the tunnel of the Métro. I pay him
a coin as hard as his notes,
and maybe he has employed me, and pays me
with his playing to hear him play.

Maybe we're necessary to each other,
and this vacant place has need of us both
—it's vacant, I mean, of dwellers,
is populated by passages and absences.

By some fate or knack he has chosen
to place his music in this cavity
where there's nothing to look at
and blindness costs him nothing.
Nothing was here before he came.

His music goes out among the sounds
of footsteps passing. The tunnel is the resonance
and meaning of what he plays.
It's his music, not the place, I go by.

In this light which is just a fact, like darkness
or the edge or end of what you may be
going toward, he turns his cap up on his knees
and leaves it there to ask and wait, and holds up
his mandolin, the lantern of his world;

his fingers make their pattern on the wires.
This is not the pursuing rhythm
of a blind cane pecking in the sun,
but is a singing in a dark place.

Dannie Abse

THREE STREET MUSICIANS

Three street musicians in mourning overcoats
worn too long, shake money boxes this morning,
then, afterwards, play their suicide notes.

The violinist in chic, black spectacles, blind,
the stout tenor with a fake Napoleon stance,
and the loony flautist following behind,

they try to importune us, the busy living,
who hear melodic snatches of music hall
above unceasing waterfalls of traffic.

Yet if anything can summon back the dead
it is the old-time sound, old obstinate tunes,
such as they achingly render and suspend:

"The Minstrel Boy," "Roses of Picardy."
No wonder cemeteries are full of silences
and stones keep down the dead that they defend.

Stones too light! Airs irresistible!
Even a dog listens, one paw raised, while the stout,
loud man amazes with nostalgic notes—though half boozed

and half clapped out. And, as breadcrumbs thrown
on the ground charm sparrows down from nowhere,
now, suddenly, there are too many ghosts about.

William Matthews

THE ACCOMPANIST

Don't play too much, don't play
too loud, don't play the melody.
You have to anticipate her
and to subdue yourself.
She used to give me her smoky
eye when I got boisterous,
so I learned to play on tip-
toe and to play the better half
of what I might. I don't like
to complain, though I notice
that I get around to it somehow.
We made a living and good music,
both, night after night, the blue
curlicues of smoke rubbing their
staling and wispy backs
against the ceilings, the flat
drinks and scarce taxis, the jazz life
we bitch about the way Army pals
complain about the food and then
re-up. Some people like to say
with smut in their voices how playing
the way we did at our best is partly
sexual. OK, I could tell them
a tale or two, and I've heard
the records Lester cut with Lady Day
and all that rap, and it's partly
sexual but it's mostly practice
and music. As for partly sexual,
I'll take wholly sexual any day,
but that's a duet and we're talking

accompaniment. Remember "Reckless
Blues"? Bessie Smith sings out "Daddy"
and Louis Armstrong plays back "Daddy"
as clear through his horn as if he'd
spoken it. But it's her daddy and her
story. When you play it you become
your part in it, one of her beautiful
troubles, and then, however much music
can do this, part of her consolation,
the way pain and joy eat off each other's
plates, but mostly you play to drunks,
to the night, to the way you judge
and pardon yourself, to all that goes
not unsung, but unrecorded.

Nils Peterson

For Charlene

Those ancients who heard the sweet sounds
Of planets' swing above the changing moon,
And the poet who wrote,
"From harmony, from heavenly harmony
This universal frame began,"
Knew something of music, how it surrounds us, impels us,
How out of its cadences, something new in us is born.
So we humans come together to sing.
We would do our best, but are not wise enough
To know what best can be.

So, bring on the conductor with her magic wand.
Let her be tall and graceful, yet stern as fate.
Let her ear be tuned to the planets
And her mind to what the words are saying.
Let her make us turn aside from the seduction of good enough.
Let her make us lose ourselves in the music.

Stand straight. Out she strides on stage. The audience applauds.
She turns to us, smiles, raises an eyebrow, then her baton. We
    begin.

Ted Hughes

CADENZA

The violinist's shadow vanishes.

The husk of a grasshopper
Sucks a remote cyclone and rises.

The full, bared throat of a woman walking water,
The loaded estuary of the dead.

And I am the cargo
Of a coffin attended by swallows.

And I am the water
Bearing the coffin that will not be silent.

The clouds are full of surgery and collision
But the coffin escapes—a black diamond,

A ruby brimming blood,
An emerald beating its shores,

The sea lifts swallow wings and flings
A summer lake open,

Sips and bewilders its reflection,
Till the whole sky dives shut like a burned land back to its
     spark—

A bat with a ghost in its mouth
Struck at by lightnings of silence—

Blue with sweat, the violinist
Crashes into the orchestra, which explodes.

D. J. Enright

SEASIDE SENSATION

The strains of an elastic band
Waft softly o'er the sandy strand.
The maestro stretches out his hands
To bless the bandiest of bands.

Their instruments are big and heavy—
A glockenspiel for spieling Glock,
A handsome, bandsome cuckoo clock,
For use in Strauss (Johann not Levi),

Deep-throated timpani in rows
For symphonics by Berlioz,
And lutes and flutes and concertinas,
Serpents, shawms and ocarinas.

The sun is shining, there are miles
Of peeling skin and healing smiles.
Also water which is doing
What it ought to, fro- and to-ing.

But can the band the bandstand stand?
Or can the bandstand stand the band?
The sand, the sand, it cannot stand
The strain of bandstand and a band!

Now swallowed up are band and stand
And smiling faces black and tanned.
The sand was quick and they were slow.
You hear them playing on below.

Kenneth Fields

Nocturne

Those other dreams, out of a former life,
Seemed to swarm at her ears as broken chords,
As music visible, a heightened world
Singing to the heart in exile—arpeggios
Lingering a little in the darkened air,
The minor calm, the dazzle, the return,
In arabesques, airy and unassailable.
Her past was living—"while, through the open window,
These cooling breezes, almost imperceptibly,
In caressing coils, in fitful eddies,
Were beginning their gentle nocturnes," Billie had played
Over and over the waltzes at Besançon,
Thought she could live forever in the fading bell
Of the tender, sad, exuberance of farewell.

Grace Schulman

The Broken String

1

When Itzhak Perlman raised his violin
and felt the string snap, he sank and looked down
at legs unfit to stand and cross the stage
for a replacement. He bowed to the maestro,
played radiant chords, and finished the concerto

with the strings he had. Rage forced low notes
as this surf crashes on rock, turns and lifts.
Later, he affirmed it's what you do:
make music with all you have, then find
a newer music with what you have left.

2

What you have left: Bill Evans at the keyboard,
Porgy. The sound rose, but one note, *unworthy,*
stalled in his head above the weightless chords,
above the bass, the trumpet's holler: *Porgy.*
A sudden clenched fist rose, pounded the keys,

fell limp: a heroin shot had hit a nerve.
I Loves You, Porgy. Sundays at the Vanguard
he soloed, improvised—his test that starved
nameless fear. Hands pitted against each other,
like the sea's crosscurrents, played away anger.

3

My father bowed before the Knabe piano,
scanned notes, touched fingers lightly, and began,
by some black art, I thought, his hearing gone
for years. And always, Mozart, Liszt, Beethoven.
One day I gasped, for there were runs

he never heard, played as a broken kite string
launches a lifelike eagle that might soar
on what the flier holds, what he has left.
Not even winds that howl along these shores
and raise the surf can ever ground that flight.

Ellen Bryant Voigt

A FUGUE

For Tom Moore, M.D.

1

The body, a resonant bowl;
the irreducible gist of wood,
that memorized the turns
of increase and relinquishing:
the held silence
where formal music will be quarried
by the cry of the strings,
the cry of the mind,
under the rosined bow.

2

The deaf listen
with compensatory hands,
touching the instrument.
Musicians also
listen, and speak, with their hands.

Such elemental implements.
The eye trains on a grid of ink,
and the fingers quicken,
habitual, learnéd,
to recover the arterial melody.

3

The long habit of living
indisposes us to dying.
In this measured space,
a drastic weeping.

————•••••————

Music depends
on its own diminishing.
Like the remembered dead,
roused from silence
and duplicated, the song heard
is sound leaving the ear.

————•••••————

Medicine too is a temporal art.
Each day, children
are rendered into your keeping.
And so you take up your instruments
to make whole, to make live,
what others made.

4

Pure science:
the cello in your lap;
the firm misleading bodies
of your own children
in your brother's room.
His illness is adult, and lethal.
You place the bow
and Beethoven turns again
from the stern physician
to annotate the page:
cantabile—

              meaning
not birdsong, windsong,
wind in the flue, bell, branch,
but the human voice,
distinct and perishable.

And you play for him.

Galway Kinnell

FAREWELL
AFTER HAYDN'S SYMPHONY IN F-SHARP MINOR

For Paul Zweig (1935–1984)

The last adagio begins.
Soon the violinist gets up and walks out.
Two cellists follow, bows erect, cellos dangling.
The flutist leaves lifting the flute high to honor it for blowing
    during all that continuous rubbing.
The bassoonist goes, then the bass fiddler.
The fortepiano player abandons the black, closeted contraption
    and walks away shaking her fingertips.
The orchestra disappears—
by ones, the way we wash up on this unmusical shore,
and by twos, the way we enter the ark where the world goes on
    beginning.
Before leaving each player blows
the glimmer off the music-stand candle,
where fireweed, dense blazing star, flame azalea stored it
    summers ago,
puffing that quantity of darkness into the hall
and the same portion of light
into the elsewhere where the players reassemble and wait
for the oboist to come with her reliable A,
as first light arrives in a beech and hemlock forest,
setting the birds sounding their chaotic vowels,
so they can tune,
and then play
the phrases inside flames wobbling on top of stalks in the field,
and in fireflies' greenish sparks of grass-sex,

and in gnats whining past in a spectral bunch,
and in crickets who would saw themselves apart to sing,
and in the golden finch perched in the mountain ash, whose
    roots push into the mouths of the emptied singers.
Now all the players have gone but two violinists,
who sit half facing each other, friends who have figured out what
    they have figured out by sounding it upon the other,
and scathe the final phrases.
By ones and twos, our powers rise and go,
until piccolos, violas, flutes, trumpets, bassoons, oboes
lie jangled up in stacks
in woodsheds waiting until a new winter
to spring again in crackling orange voices; and only two are left.
In the darkness above the stage I imagine
the face of my old friend Paul Zweig
—who went away, his powers intact, into Eternity's Woods alone,
    under a double singing of birds—
looking down and saying something like
"Let the limits of knowing stretch and diaphanise,
so that life includes more and more death.
Knowledge increasing into ignorance gives the falling-trajectory
    its grace."
The bow-hairs still cast dust on the bruised wood.
Everything on earth, born
only moments ago, abruptly tips over
and is dragged by mistake into the chaotic inevitable.
Goodbye, dear friend.
Even the meantime, which is the holy time
of being on earth in the overlapping lifetimes, ends.
This is one of its endings.

The violinists scrape one more time,
the last of the adagio flies out through the f-holes.
The audience straggles from the hall and at once disappears.
For myself I go on foot on Seventh Avenue
down to the little, bent streets of the West Village.
From ahead of me comes the *hic* of somebody drunk
and then the *nunc* of his head bumping against the telephone
    pole.

Contributors' Notes

DANNIE ABSE (b. 1923) is a Welsh poet, playwright, essayist, and novelist, as well as a physician. He is the author and editor of numerous books of poetry, among them *After Every Green Thing* and *White Coat, Purple Coat: Collected Poems 1948–1988.*

DIANE ACKERMAN (b. 1956) is a poet, essayist, and naturalist. She is the author of many highly acclaimed works of nonfiction, including the bestselling *A Natural History of the Senses, Cultivating Delight,* and, most recently, *An Alchemy of Mind.*

FLEUR ADCOCK (b. 1934), a New Zealander by birth, lives in London. She is the author of ten books of poetry, including *Poems 1960–2000.* Recipient of the Cholmondeley Award in 1976 and a New Zealand National Book Award in 1984, she was awarded an OBE in 1996.

W. H. AUDEN (1907–73), one of the major figures of twentieth-century poetry, wrote several libretti in collaboration with Chester Kallman, among them one for Igor Stravinsky's *The Rake's Progress.*

MATSUO BASHŌ (1644–1694) is considered the greatest of the Japanese *haiku* poets, a form influenced by Zen Buddhism and to which he gave new freedom and energy.

CHARLES BAUDELAIRE (1821–1867) wrote *Les Fleurs du Mal* (1857), a pillar of nineteenth-century verse.

WENDELL BERRY (b. 1934), a Kentuckian, is an eloquent spokesman for conservation and sustainable agriculture, topics he has pursued in over thirty books of essays, poetry, and fiction, including *The Unsettling of America, Home Economics: Eighteen Essays,* and *A Timbered Choir.*

JILL BIALOSKY (b. 1957) is an editor at W. W. Norton and Company, the author of two books of poetry, *The End of Desire* and *Subterranean,* and co-editor of an anthology, *Wanting a Child.*

ELIZABETH BISHOP (1911–1979) is a major figure of twentieth-century poetry. She won numerous awards and honors in her lifetime, among them the Pulitzer Prize and the National Book Critics Circle Award.

PAUL BLACKBURN (1926–1971) published thirteen books of original poetry, as well as translations from the Spanish and the Provençal.

ROBERT BLY (b. 1926), the son of Norwegian farmers, is a prolific and award-winning poet, translator, and editor. He is author of the bestselling *Iron John: A Book About Men*, and over 40 collections of poetry, most recently *My Sentence Was a Thousand Years of Joy.*

LOUISE BOGAN (1897–1970) was poetry editor of *The New Yorker* for 38 years. Her books of poems include *Body of This Death*, *Dark Summer*, and *The Blue Estuaries: Poems 1923–1968*. She served as Consultant in Poetry (now Poet Laureate) at the Library of Congress in 1945–46, and she was awarded the Bollingen Prize in 1968.

EAVAN BOLAND (b. 1944) was born in Dublin, Ireland, and is currently Professor in Humanities at Stanford University. Her volumes of poetry include *Against Love Poetry*, *Outside History: Selected Poems (1980–1990)*, and *Domestic Violence.*

BRUCE BOND (b. 1954) earned a Masters in Music Performance from Lamont School of Music. His books of poetry include *Independence Days*, *The Anteroom of Paradise*, *Radiography*, *The Throats of Narcissus*, and *Cinder*. Director of creative writing at the University of North Texas, he performs classical and jazz guitar in the Dallas area.

YVES BONNEFOY (b. 1923) is one of France's most celebrated writers. He has translated the plays of Shakespeare and published seven books of poetry, including *On the motion and immobility of Douve*, and several books of criticism. He was awarded the Prix Goncourt for Poetry in 1987.

EDGAR BOWERS (1924–2000) taught at the University of California at Santa Barbara. Among his many awards were two Guggenheim Fellowships and the Bollingen Prize for Poetry. His books of poems include *The Astronomers* and *Collected Poems*.

GABRIELLE CALVOCORESSI (b. 1974) is the author of *The Last Time I Saw Amelia Earhart*, which won the 2006 Connecticut Book Award in Poetry.

HAYDEN CARRUTH (b. 1921) is a poet associated with jazz and the blues. His plethora of poetry collections includes *Collected Longer Poems*, *Collected Shorter Poems*, *Scrambled Eggs and Whiskey*, and his long poem, *The Sleeping Beauty.*

NICHOLAS CHRISTOPHER (b. 1951) is the author of eight volumes of poetry, including *Atomic Field: Two Poems, The Creation of the Night Sky*, and *Crossing the Equator,* as well as five novels and a book about film noir, *Somewhere in the Night.*

LEONARD COHEN (b. 1934) is a poet, novelist, and one of the most influential songwriters of the late-twentieth century.

BILLY COLLINS (b. 1941) served as Poet Laureate of the United States from 2001 to 2003. A jazz pianist, he has written eloquently about music. His most recent book is *The Trouble with Poetry and Other Poems.*

HENRI COULETTE (1927–1988) wrote two collections of poetry, *The War of the Secret Agents*, which was a Lamont Poetry Selection of the Academy of American Poets, and *The Family Goldschmitt.*

DICK DAVIS (b. 1945) graduated from King's College, Cambridge. He returned to England after ten years in Iran in 1978, and emerged as one of Britain's foremost translators of Persian poetry. Volumes of his own poetry include *Touchwood, A New Kind of Love, Devices and Desires,* and *Covenant.*

EMILY DICKINSON (1830–1886) is one of the most important figures in the history of American poetry. Of her 1,789 surviving poems, only eleven were published in her lifetime.

STEPHEN DOBYNS (b. 1941) is the author of twelve books of poetry and a number of novels, including a popular series of detective books, the Bradshaw mysteries. His most recent book of poems is *Mystery, So Long.*

MARK DOTY (b. 1953) is the author of seven poetry collections, among them *School of the Arts*; *Atlantis*, which received the Ambassador Book Award, the Bingham Poetry Prize, and a Lambda Literary Award; and *My Alexandria*, which won the National Book Critics Circle Award and Britain's T. S. Eliot Prize.

CAROL MUSKE-DUKES (b. 1945) is a poet, novelist, essayist, critic, and the founder and director of the graduate program in literature and creative writing at the University of Southern California. Her latest collection of poetry, *Sparrow*, was a finalist for The National Book Award.

CORNELIUS EADY (b. 1954) is the author of several books of poetry, among them *Victims of the Latest Dance Craze, The Gathering of My Name,* and *You Don't Miss Your Water.* He has received fellowships from the Guggenheim Foundation, the National Endowment for the Arts, the Rockefeller Foundation, and the Lila Wallace-Reader's Digest Foundation.

D. J. ENRIGHT (1920–2002) was born and educated in England. His output over his long life included novels, essays, and entertaining memoir, as well as poetry. In 1981 he was awarded the Queens Gold Medal for Poetry.

B. H. FAIRCHILD (b. 1942) grew up in small towns in west Texas, Oklahoma, and Kansas. He is the author of three books of poetry, including *The Art of the Lathe*, winner of the Kingsley Tufts Award, the William Carlos Williams Award, the California Book Award, and the PEN Center West Poetry Award.

KENNETH FIELDS (b. 1939) is the author of a number of poetry collections, including *The Other Walker, Sunbelly, The Odysseus Manuscript, Anemographia, A Treatise on the Wind,* and *Classic Rough News.*

JANE FLANDERS (b. 1940) is the author of the poetry collections *Leaving and Coming Back, The Students of Snow, Timepiece,* and *Sudden Plenty.*

ROBERT FROST (1847–1963) was the most widely read and admired American poet of the twentieth century. He won three Pulitzer Prizes for his work and was appointed Consultant in Poetry in English (now Poet Laureate) at the Library of Congress.

DANA GIOIA (b. 1950) is a prolific poet, essayist, reviewer, editor, and translator, and librettist of the opera *Nosferatu.* His critical collection, *Can Poetry Matter?,* was a finalist for the National Book Critics Circle Award. He is currently Chairman of the National Endowment of the Arts.

LOUISE GLÜCK (b. 1943) is the author of nine books of poetry and one collection of essays, *Proofs and Theories: Essays on Poetry.* She has received the Pulitzer Prize, the National Book Critics Circle Award for Poetry, the William Carlos Williams Award, and the PEN/Martha Albrand Award for Nonfiction. She was U.S. poet laureate in 2004.

JENNIFER GROTZ (b. 1971) is the author of *Cusp,* which won the 2002 Bakeless Prize. Since then, she has become Assistant Director of the Bread Loaf Writers Conference.

CHARLES GULLANS (1929–1993) was a poet and translator. His critically acclaimed *Arrivals and Departures* was the first of six volumes of poetry. *Letter from Los Angeles,* the final volume, appeared in 1990.

LARS GUSTAFSSON (b. 1936) is one of Sweden's leading men of letters. He is known in the English-speaking world primarily for his novels and short stories, but he is also the author of more than ten distinguished books of poetry.

DANIEL HALL (b. 1952) is the author of three books of poems: *Hermit with Landscape* (which won the Yale Younger Poets Prize), *Strange Relation,* and *Under Sleep.* He is presently the writer-in-residence at Amherst College.

MARY STEWART HAMMOND (b. 1947) is the author of *Out of Canaan,* which received the 1992 Best First Collection of Poetry Award from the Great Lakes Colleges Association.

THOMAS HARDY (1840–1928), the renowned novelist and poet, wrote a number of poems on musical themes; his father and grandfather sang in the local church choir, and Hardy was, in his youth, an ardent fiddle player.

MICHAEL S. HARPER (b. 1938) is an editor of *The Viking Book of African American Poetry* and the author of several books of poetry, among them *Dear John, Dear Coltrane,* and *Honorable Amendments.*

TERRANCE HAYES (b. 1971) is the author of *Wind in a Box, Hip Logic,* and *Muscular Music.* He is a professor of English at Carnegie-Mellon University.

SEAMUS HEANEY (b. 1939) is from County Derry, Northern Ireland. His books include *Selected Poems 1965–1975, Government of the Tongue, The Redress of Poetry, Opened Ground: Poems 1966–1996.* He was awarded the Nobel Prize for Literature in 1972. His best-selling translation of *Beowulf* won the Whitbread Award.

ANTHONY HECHT (1923–2004) is the author of seven books of poetry, including *The Hard Hours,* which received the Pulitzer Prize in 1968. He is also the author of several volumes of essays and criticism. His many awards include the Bollingen Prize in Poetry, the Eugenio Montale Award, the Wallace Stevens Award, and the Robert Frost Medal.

ROBERT HERRICK (1591–1674) was one of a group of Cavalier Poets centered around an admiration of Ben Jonson. His best known collections of lyric poetry *Hesperides* and *Noble Numbers,* both published in 1684.

EDWARD HIRSCH (b. 1950) has written six books of poems, including *Wild Gratitude*, which won the National Book Critics Circle Award, and three prose books, including *How to Read a Poem and Fall in Love With Poetry*, a national bestseller. He has received the Prix de Rome and a MacArthur Fellowship and is President of the John Simon Guggenheim Memorial Foundation.

TONY HOAGLAND (b. 1953) is the author of three books of poetry: *Sweet Ruin*, which won the Brittingham Prize in Poetry; *Donkey Gospel*, which received the 1997 James Laughlin Award of The Academy of American Poets; and *What Narcissism Means to Me*.

JOHN HOLLANDER (b. 1929) has written many volumes of poetry, including *Picture Window, Tesserae*, and *A Crackling of Thorns*, as well as seven books of criticism. He has also edited numerous anthologies, including the bestselling *Committed to Memory: 100 Best Poems to Memorize*, and has received a Bollingen Prize and a MacArthur Fellowship. He is Sterling Professor of English at Yale University.

BILL HOLM (b. 1943) divides his time between a farm north of Minneota, Minnesota, and a northern Iceland fjord, where he writes and practices the piano. Among his nine books of poetry and essays are *Coming Home Crazy, Eccentric Islands, Playing the Black Piano*, and *The Dead Get By with Everything*.

RICHARD HOWARD (b. 1929) is a poet, scholar, teacher, critic, and translator. The author of more than a dozen books of poetry and criticism, including *Inner Voices: Selected Poems, 1963–2003* and *Paper Trail: Selected Prose, 1965–2003*, he is the recipient of numerous awards and honors, including the Pulitzer Prize.

DAVID HUDDLE (b. 1942) lives in Vermont, where he writes fiction and essays as well as poetry. Among his publications are the book of poems *Grayscale* and the novel *The Story of a Million Years*.

TED HUGHES (1930–1998) was a distinguished author of poetry, plays, and children's literature. He was Poet Laureate of England from 1984 until his death.

ISSA (1763–1827) was one of the foremost poets of the Japanese haiku tradition.

ROLF JACOBSEN (1907–1994), the Norwegian poet who was an early champion of modernism, published a body of work that established him as one of Europe's great poets.

DONALD JUSTICE (1925–2004) played clarinet and piano as a teenager and studied musical composition with Carl Ruggles at the University of Miami. His *Selected Poems* received the Pulitzer Prize in 1979.

BRIGIT PEGEEN KELLY (b. 1951) is the author of *The Orchard Song*, the 1994 Lamont Poetry Selection of The Academy of American Poets, and *To The Place of Trumpets*, selected for the Yale Series of Younger Poets.

JACK KEROUAC (1922–1969), author of *On the Road* and many other books, was a leader and spokesperson for the Beat Movement in American poetry, which was centered in San Francisco.

GALWAY KINNELL (b. 1927) has been a MacArthur Fellow and the state poet of Vermont. He has won the Pulitzer Prize and the National Book Award and has published several books of translations. For many years he was the Erich Maria Remarque Professor of Creative Writing at New York University. His latest collection of poetry is entitled *Strong Is Your Hold*.

SUSAN KINSOLVING (b. 1946) is the author of three collections of poetry, *Among Flowers, Rushes & Dailies*, and *The White Eyelash*. She has taught at California Institute of the Arts and the University of Connecticut.

KENNETH KOCH (1925–2002) published many volumes of poetry, most recently *A Possible World* and *New Addresses*, plays, and fiction. He also wrote several books about poetry, including *Wishes, Lies, and Dreams; Rose, Where Did You Get That Red?;* and *Making Your Own Days: The Pleasures of Reading and Writing Poetry*.

WAYNE KOESTENBAUM (b. 1958) was co-winner of the 1989 "Discovery"/*The Nation* contest. He is the author of four collections of poems, as well as a number of books of cultural studies, among them *The Queen's Throat: Opera, Homosexuality, and the Mystery of Desire*.

YUSEF KOMUNYAKAA (b. 1947) was awarded the Bronze Star for his service in Vietnam, where he was a correspondent and managing editor of the *Southern Cross*. His books of poetry include *Copacetic; I Apologize for the Eyes in My Head; Neon Vernacular: New and Selected Poems*, which won the Pulitzer Prize; and *Thieves of Paradise*.

LOUISE LABÉ (c. 1520–1566) was a French poet of the Renaissance, educated in Latin, Italian, and music. Her *Euvres* were printed in 1555 by the renowned Lyonnais printer, Jean de Tournes. In 1557 a popular song about her was also published.

DORIANNE LAUX (b. 1952) as a single mother, worked as a gas station manager, sanatorium cook, maid, and donut holer until, supported by scholarships and grants, she returned to school and graduated from Mills College. Among her books of poetry are *Awake, Smoke,* and *What We Carry.*

D. H. LAWRENCE (1885–1930) is author of many celebrated novels, including *Sons and Lovers* and *Lady Chatterley's Lover.* His fame as a novelist tends to overshadow the fact that he is one of the major British poets of the twentieth century.

LI-YOUNG LEE (b. 1957) is the author of *Book of My Nights, The City in Which I Love You,* and *Rose,* which won the Delmore Schwartz Memorial Poetry Award. His memoir, *The Winged Seed: A Remembrance,* received an American Book Award.

DAVID LEHMAN (b. 1948) has written seven books of poetry, among them *The Daily Mirror, The Evening Sun,* and *When a Woman Loves a Man.* He is the series editor of *The Best American Poetry,* the anthology he established in 1988.

PHILIP LEVINE (b. 1928) is the author of sixteen collections of poems, most recently *Breath,* and two books of essays. He is the recipient of two National Book Awards—for *Ashes* and *What Work Is*—and the Pulitzer Prize for *The Simple Truth.*

FEDERICO GARCÍA LORCA (1898–1936) was a Spanish poet and dramatist born in Andalusia and murdered by the Nationalists soon after the outbreak of the civil war.

AMY LOWELL (1874–1925) edited an annual anthology, *Some Imagist Poets,* and published several collections of poetry, two critical works, a volume of Chinese translations, and a biography, *John Keats.* Her posthumous publication, *What's O'Clock,* won the Pulitzer Prize for poetry in 1926.

MINA LOY (1882–1966) published a short-lived Dadaist journal, *The Blind Man,* with Marcel Duchamp. Her selected poems were published as *The Lost Lunar Baedeker.*

WILLIAM MATTHEWS (1942–1997) published eleven books of poetry, including *Time & Money,* which won the National Book

Critics Circle Award. He received many awards, including the Ruth Lilly Poetry prize.

J. D. McCLATCHY (b. 1945) is a much-honored poet, critic, and editor. He is also a renowned librettist who has collaborated with composers such as William Schumann, Francis Thorne, Ned Rorem, Lorin Maazel, Lowell Liebermann, and Elliot Goldenthal. His libretto for Mozart's *The Magic Flute* recently debuted at the Metropolitan Opera.

SANDRA McPHERSON (b. 1943) is a professor of English at the University of California at Davis. Her books of poems include *The Year of Our Birth, Floralia, The God of Indeterminacy,* and *A Visit to Civilization.*

WILLIAM MEREDITH (b. 1919) served in the U.S. Navy, where he received medals for flying carrier planes. He has worked as opera critic, dramatist, translator, editor, public servant, and poet. *Partial Accounts: New and Selected Poems* won the Pulitzer Prize.

JAMES MERRILL (1926–1995), one of the major American poets of the twentieth century, wrote twelve books of poems, among them *Nights and Days*, which received the National Book Award, and *Divine Comedies*, which won the Pulitzer Prize in 1976. His numerous awards included the Bollingen Prize for Poetry in 1973.

W. S. MERWIN (b. 1927) is a poet and translator. His many awards include the Pulitzer Prize, the Tanning Prize for mastery in the art of poetry, and the Bollingen Award. He has served as a Chancellor of the Academy of American Poets, and he is the author of dozens of books, including *Migration: New & Selected Poems.*

EDNA ST. VINCENT MILLAY (1892–1950) won instant acclaim at the age of twenty with the publication of her long poem "Renascence." A mainstay of bohemian Greenwich Village in the 1920s, she authored many books of poems and verse dramas, and *The Ballad of the Harp Weaver* won the Pulitzer Prize. She also wrote the libretto to the opera *The King's Henchmen,* which debuted at the Metropolitan Opera in 1927.

CZESLAW MILOSZ (1911–2004) was awarded the Nobel Prize for Literature in 1980. Most of his poems were written in his native Polish, though many were later translated into English with such poets as Robert Hass and Robert Pinsky.

EUGENIO MONTALE (1896–1981), widely acknowledged as the greatest Italian poet since Leopardi, was also a voluminous writer of prose stories as well as cultural, literary, and music criticism and a talented amateur painter. Montale was awarded the Nobel Prize in Literature in 1975.

LISEL MUELLER (1924) came to the United States to flee the Nazis when she was fifteen. Her books of poetry include *Alive Together: New and Selected Poems*, which won the Pulitzer Prize, and *The Need to Hold Still*, which received the National Book Award.

OGDEN NASH (1902–1971) is the author of numerous volumes of light verse and children's verse, including *Hard Lines*, *Happy Days*, and *Bed Riddance: A Posy for the Indisposed*. He was librettist of the Broadway musical hit, *One Touch of Venus*.

HOWARD NEMEROV (1920–1991) wrote fiction, plays, poetry, and criticism, and his *Collected Poems* (1977) won the Pulitzer Prize. He was a Chancellor of the Academy of American Poets, and from 1988–1990 the Poet Laureate of the United States.

PABLO NERUDA (1904–1973), who received the 1971 Nobel Prize for Literature, is one of the most important poets of the twentieth century. His books, written in his native Spanish, include *Twenty Love Poems and a Song of Despair*, *One Hundred Love Sonnets*, *The Captain's Verses*, *Odes to Common Things*, and *The Heights of Machu Pichu*.

NAOMI SHIHAB NYE (b. 1952) has received numerous awards for her poetry as well as for her books for younger readers. She has been a Lannan Fellow, a Guggenheim Fellow, and a Witter Bynner Fellow.

FRANK O'HARA (1926–1966) was a fine piano player who studied and composed music before beginning to write poetry. He was also a renowned art critic who served as a curator and catalog writer at the Museum of Modern Art in New York City. His eight books of poetry include *Mediations in an Emergency* and *Lunch Poems*.

MARY OLIVER (b. 1925) has published numerous books of poetry and five books of prose. *American Primitive* received the Pulitzer Prize in Poetry and *New and Selected Poems* won the National Book Award in 1992.

LINDA PASTAN (b. 1923) is the author of eleven works of poetry, including *Queen of a Rainy Country*, *The Last Uncle*, *Carnival Evening: New and Selected Poems 1968–1998*, and *An Early Afterlife*. In 2003 she received the Ruth Lilly Poetry Prize.

NILS PETERSON (b. 1933) has published poetry, science fiction, and articles on subjects from golf to Shakespeare. His poetry collections include *Here Is No Ordinary Rejoicing, The Comedy of Desire,* and *Driving a Herd of Moose to Durango.*

ROBERT PHILLIPS (b. 1938) is the author or editor of some 30 volumes of poetry, fiction, criticism, and *belles lettres* and publishes in numerous journals. His most recent books of poems are *News About People You Know* and *Circumstances Beyond Our Control.*

ROBERT PINSKY (b. 1940) founded the Favorite Poem Project during his tenure as the Poet Laureate of the United States. He is the author of numerous books of poetry, most recently *Jersey Rain.*

VASKO POPA (1922–1991), a modernist influenced by French surrealism and Serbian folk traditions, was one of Eastern Europe's foremost poets. He was born in the former Yugoslavia and lived in Belgrade.

ANNE PORTER (b. 1911) co-wrote and starred in Rudy Burckhardt's film, *A Day in the Life of a Cleaning Woman* (1953). She published poems in numerous magazines and has authored *An Altogether Different Language* and *Living Things.*

CARL RAKOSI (b. 1903–2004) was the last surviving member of the Objectivist poets. He was still publishing and performing his poetry well into his nineties.

LIAM RECTOR (b. 1949) is the author of three books of poetry, including *The Sorrow of Architecture.* He edited *The Day I Was Older: On the Poetry of Donald Hall* and co-edited *On the Poetry of Frank Bidart: Fastening the Voice to the Page.*

CHRISTINA GEORGINA ROSSETTI (1830–1894) was never completely a part of the Pre-Raphaelite Brotherhood, but her *Goblin Market and Other Poems* (1862) was its first unalloyed literary success.

RUMI (1207–1273) was born in Afghanistan, which was then part of the Persian Empire. A religious scholar, he left his position of sheikh in the Dervish learning community in Konya after a transformative meeting and subsequent friendship with the wandering Dervish, Shams of Tabriz. It was only after Shams's mysterious disappearance that Rumi began writing the great number of poems for which he is known today.

MURIEL RUKEYSER (1913–1980) worked in Spain as a journalist at the time of the Spanish Civil War. She later taught at Sarah Lawrence College. She wrote prose and children's books, and she translated the poems of Octavio Paz. Her *Collected Poems* appeared in 1978.

MICHAEL RYAN (b. 1946) has written four books of poetry, an auto-biography, a memoir, and a collection of essays about poetry and writing. His awards include the Lenore Marshall Poetry Prize, a Whiting Writers Award, and the Yale Series of Younger Poets Award.

SAPPHO (c. 630–570 B.C.) was one of the great Greek lyricists and few known female poets of the ancient world. She composed her own music, and her poems were performed with the accompani-ment of a lyre. The bulk of her poetry has been lost, but her reputa-tion is immense.

MAY SARTON (1912–1995) wrote over fifty books of poetry and prose, including *A Walk Through the Woods, A World of Light, Writings on Writing,* and *The Magnificent Spinster.*

SIEGFRIED SASSOON (1886–1967) is best known for his war poems and for his nonfiction volumes, *Memoirs of a Fox Hunting Man* and *Siegfried's Journey.*

PETER SCHMITT (b. 1958) is the author of *Country Airport* and *Hazard Duty.* His awards include a 1988 Discovery Prize from *The Nation* and an Ingram Merrill Fellowship.

GRACE SCHULMAN (b. 1935)) is author of a number of poetry col-lections, including *The Broken String, Days of Wonder: New and Selected Poems,* and *The Paintings of Our Lives.* Recipient of many awards and fellowships, she is editor of *The Poems of Marianne Moore* and Distinguished Professor of English at Baruch College.

DELMORE SCHWARTZ (1913–1966) won the Bollingen Poetry Prize in 1959 for his poetry collection *Summer Knowledge: New and Selected Poems.*

HARVEY SHAPIRO (b. 1924) has written many books, including *How Charlie Shavers Died and Other Poems* and *National Cold Storage Company.* He has served as editor of *The New York Times Book Review* and as senior editor of *The New York Times Magazine.*

JOHN SMITH (b. 1924) is a British poet whose book, *Selected Poems,* was published in 1982.

WILLIAM JAY SMITH (b. 1918) is the author of more than fifty books of poetry, children's verse, literary criticism, translation, and mem-oirs, and editor of several influencial anthologies. He served as Consultant in Poetry to the Library of Congress (now Poet Laureate) from 1968–1970.

WALLACE STEVENS (1879–1955) was one of the major American poets of the twentieth century. He received the Bollingen Prize in 1950 and the National Book Award in 1951, and a second National Book Award and the Pulitzer Prize for his *Collected Poems* in 1955.

WISLAWA SZYMBORSKA (b. 1923) is a native of Poland and one of the world's most renowned poets. She has worked as a poetry editor, a columnist, and a translator and has published more than fifteen books of poetry. She was awarded the Nobel Prize for Literature in 1996.

HENRY TAYLOR (b. 1924) is a teacher, horseman, poet, and parodist. He received the Pulitzer Prize in 1986 for his third book of poems, *The Flying Change*. His other poetry collections are *Brief Candles: 101 Clerihews*; *Understanding Fiction*, *The Horse Show at Midnight* and *An Afternoon of Billiards*.

CHARLES TOMLINSON (b. 1927) is a poet, translator, critic, university professor, and artist. He is the recipient of numerous prizes and awards, including the Bennett Award, and is a member of the American Academy of Arts and Sciences and the British CBE.

TOMAS TRANSTRÖMER (b. 1931) was born and educated in Stockholm. He has written eleven books of poems and is the recipient of such honors as the Neustadt International Prize for Literature, the Bonnier Award for Poetry, Germany's Petrarch Prize, and the Swedish Academy's Nordic Prize.

CHUANG TZU (c. 369–268 B.C.) was one of China's greatest poets and prose writers. A leading thinker representing the Taoist strain in Chinese thought, he set forth the early ideas of what was to become the Taoist School

JOHN UPDIKE (b. 1932) has written many novels, including *The Centaur* and the *Rabbit* quadrology. He is also the author of seven books of poetry and the winner of numerous awards, including two Pulitzer Prizes and the National Medal of the Arts.

ELLEN BRYANT VOIGT (b. 1943) has published seven volumes of poetry, including *Messenger: New and Selected Poems* and *Kyrie*. She is co-editor of an anthology of essays, *Poets Teaching Poets: Self and the World* and collected her own essays on craft in *The Flexible Lyric*.

DEREK WALCOTT (b. 1930) was born on the island of St. Lucia. He taught for many years in the United States and was awarded the

Nobel Prize for Literature in 1992. His publications include *Omeiros* and *The Bounty.*

KENNETH WEISNER (b. 1955) teaches English and Creative Writing at De Anza College. The author of *The Sacred Geometry of Pedestrians*, he lives in Santa Cruz, California, with the pianist Kit Birskovich.

SUSAN WHEELER (b. 1955) is the author of four collections of poetry, most recently *Ledger,* and a novel, *Record Palace*, which is set in a jazz record shop in Chicago.

JAMES WRIGHT (1927–1980) won many honors for his poetry, including the Yale Younger Poets Award and the Pulitzer Prize. His book *The Branch Shall Not Break*, published in 1963, was considered a major breakthrough in American poetry.

KEVIN YOUNG (b. 1970) is the author of five books of poems, including *Black Maria, Jelly Roll*, and *To Repel Ghosts [The Remix].* He is the editor of *Giant Steps: The New Generation of African American Writers Blues Poems*, and most recently, *John Berryman: Selected Poems* (2004).

ADAM ZAGAJEWSKI (b. 1945) is one of Poland's most famous contemporary poets as well as a novelist and essayist. Among his recent books in English is *Mysticism for Beginners.* He lives in Paris and Houston.

JAN ZWICKY (b. 1955) is a Canadian philosopher, poet, essayist, and violinist. Among her publications are seven books of poetry, including *Songs for Relinquishing the Earth* and, most recently, *Thirty-seven Small Songs & Thirteen Silences* (2005). Her books of philosophy are *Lyric Philosophy* and *Wisdom & Metaphor.*

Acknowledgments

Dannie Abse: "Three Street Musicians." Reprinted by permission of The Peters Fraser and Dunlop Group Ltd. on behalf of Dannie Abse. From *Collected Poems* (Hutchinson), copyright © 1977 by Dannie Abse.

Diane Ackerman: "Rachmaninoff's Psychiatrist" from *Origami Bridges: Poems of Psychoanalysis and Fire* by Diane Ackerman. Copyright © 2002 by Diane Ackerman. Reprinted by permission of HarperCollins Publishers.

Fleur Adcock: "Piano Concerto in E Flat Major" from *Poems 1960–2000*. Copyright © 2000 by Fleur Adcock. Reprinted by permission of Bloodaxe Books Ltd.

W. H. Auden: "The Composer" copyright © 1976 by Edward Mendelson, William Meredith and Monroe K. Spears, Executors of the Estate of W. H. Auden, from *Collected Poems* by W. H. Auden. Used by permission of Random House, Inc.

Matsuo Bashō: [The temple bell], translated by Robert Bly. Copyright © by Robert Bly. Reprinted by kind permission of the translator.

Charles Baudelaire: "Music: Beethoven" from *Les Fleurs du mal*. Copyright © 1982 by Charles Baudelaire. Translated from the French by Richard Howard, Illustrations by Michael Mazur. Reprinted by permission of David R. Godine, Publisher, Inc.

Wendell Berry: "A Music" from *Collected Poems: 1957–1982*. Copyright © 1985 by Wendell Berry. Reprinted by permission of North Point Press, a division of Farrar, Straus and Giroux, LLC.

Jill Bialosky: "Music Lesson" from *Subterranean: Poems* by Jill Bialosky. Copyright © 2001 by Jill Bialosky. Used by permission of Alfred A. Knopf, a division of Random House, Inc.

Elizabeth Bishop: "Sonnet" from *The Complete Poems 1927–1979*. Copyright © 1979, 1983 by Alice Helen Methfessel. Reprinted by permission of Farrar, Straus and Giroux, LLC.

Paul Blackburn: "Listening to Sonny Rollins" from *Poems of Paul Blackburn*. Copyright ©1985 by Joan Blackburn. Reprinted by kind permission of Persea Books.

Robert Bly: "Listening to the Köln Concert" reprinted from *Eating the Honey of Words: New and Selected Poems*, HarperCollins Publishers, New York, 1999, copyright © 1999 by Robert Bly. Reprinted by kind permission of the author.

Louise Bogan: "Musician" from *The Blue Estuaries*. Copyright © 1968 by Louise Bogan. Copyright renewed 1996 by Ruth Limmer. Reprinted by permission of Farrar, Straus and Giroux, LLC.

Eavan Boland: "Fond Memory" from *Outside History: Selected Poems 1980–1990* by Eavan Boland, copyright © 1990 by Eavan Boland. Used by permission of W. W. Norton & Company, Inc.

Bruce Bond: "Thelonious Sphere Monk" from *The Throats of Narcissus*, copyright © 2001 by Bruce Bond. Reprinted with the permission of the University of Arkansas Press.

Yves Bonnefoy: "To the Voice of Kathleen Ferrier" from *New and Selected Poems*, edited by John Naughton and Anthony Rudolf, copyright 1958 © University of Chicago Press. Reprinted by permission of University of Chicago Press.

Edgar Bowers: "From J. Haydn to Constanze Mozart" from *Collected Poems* by Edgar Bowers, copyright © 1997 by Edgar Bowers. Used by permission of Alfred A. Knopf, a division of Random House, Inc.

Gabrielle Calvocoressi: "A Love Supreme," copyright © by Gabrielle Calvocoressi. Used by kind permission of the author.

Nicholas Christopher: "Jazz" from *Crossing the Equator: New & Selected Poems 1972–2004*. Copyright © 2004 by Nicholas Christopher. Reprinted by kind permission of Harcourt, Inc., and the author.

Hayden Carruth: "Billie Holliday" from *Collected Shorter Poems 1946-1991*. Copyright © 1989 by Hayden Carruth. Reprinted with permission of Copper Canyon Press. "All Things," from *The Oldest Killed Lake in North America* (Salt-Works Press, 1985), copyright © by Hayden Carruth. Reprinted by kind permission of the author.

Chuang Tzu: "The Breath of Nature" from *The Way of Chuang Tzu* by Thomas Merton. Copyright © 1965 by The Abbey of Gethsemani. Reprinted by permission of New Directions Publishing Corporation.

Leonard Cohen: "His Master's Voice" from *Book of Longing* (New York: The Ecco Press, 2006), copyright © 2006 by Leonard Cohen. Reprinted with permission of HarperCollins Publishers.

Billy Collins: "Sunday Morning with the Sensational Nightingales"; "Piano Lessons" and "Nightclub" from *The Art of Drowning*, copyright 1995 © by Billy Collins. Reprinted by permission of the University of Pittsburgh Press.

Henri Coulette: excerpt from "Epigrams" from *The Collected Poems of Henri Coulette*, edited by Donald Justice and Robert Mezey, copyright © 1990.

Guy Davenport: "Sappho: III" from *7 Greeks*, copyright © 1995 by Guy Davenport. Reprinted by permission of New Directions Publishing Corp.

Dick Davis: "Listening" from *A Trick of Sunlight* (Swallow Press/Ohio University Press, 2006), copyright © Dick Davis. Reprinted with the permission of Ohio University Press/Swallow Press, Athens, Ohio.

Emily Dickinson: "I shall keep singing!" and "Heart not so heavy as mine" by permission of the publishers and Trustees of Amherst College from *The*

Louise Labé: "The Twelfth Sonnet" translated by Frederic Prokosch, from *The Sonnets of Louise Labé*. Copyright © 1947 by New Directions Publishing Corp. Reprinted by permission of New Directions Publishing Corp.

Dorianne Laux: "The Ebony Chickering" and "Singing Back the World" from *What We Carry*. Copyright © 1994 By Dorianne Laux. Reprinted with the permission of BOA Editions, Ltd.

Li-Young Lee: "I Ask My Mother to Sing" from *Rose*. Copyright © 1986 by Li-Young Lee. Reprinted with the permission of BOA Editions, Ltd.

David Lehman: "Radio" from *When a Woman Loves a Man*. Copyright © 2005 by David Lehman. Reprinted by permission of Writers' Representatives, LLC.

Philip Levine: "Songs" from *Ashes* (Atheneum, 1979). Reprinted by kind permission of the author.

Li Yi: "On Hearing a Flute at Night" translated by Witter Bynner, from *The Jade Mountain*, translated by Witter Bynner. Copyright © 1929 by Alfred A. Knopf, a division of Random House, Inc. Used by permission of Alfred A. Knopf, a division of Random House, Inc.

Federico García Lorca: "The Guitar" translated by Christopher Maurer, from *In Search of Duende*. Copyright © 1955, 1998 by New Directions Publishing Corp. Copyright © Herederos de Federico García Lorca, translation © Christopher Maurer and Herederos de Federico García Lorca. Reprinted by permission of New Directions Publishing Corp.

Amy Lowell: "An Opera House" from *The Complete Poetical Works of Amy Lowell*. Copyright © 1955 by Houghton Mifflin Company. Renewed 1983 by Houghton Mifflin Company, Brinton P. Roberts and G. D'Andelot Belin, Esq. Reprinted by permission of Houghton Mifflin Company. All rights reserved.

Mina Loy: "Stravinski's Flute," from *The Last Lunar Baedeker*. Copyright © 1982, estate of Mina Loy. Courtesy of Roger L. Conover.

Thomas Lux: "Regarding (Most) Songs" from *The Street of Clocks: Poems*. Copyright © 2001 by Thomas Lux. Reprinted by permission of Houghton Mifflin Company. All rights reserved.

William Matthews: "Va, Pensiero" from *Time and Money: New Poems*. Copyright © 1995 by William Matthews. Reprinted by permission of Houghton Mifflin Company. "The Accompanist" from *Foreseeable Futures: Poems*. Copyright © 1987 by William Matthews. Reprinted by permission of Houghton Mifflin Company. All rights reserved.

J. D. McClatchy: "Night Piece" from *The Rest of The Way*, by J. D. McClatchy. Copyright © 1990 by J. D. McClatchy. Used by permission of Alfred A. Knopf, a division of Random House, Inc. "My Old Idols; Section II: Callas" from *Ten Commandments*, by J. D. McClatchy. Copyright © 1998 by J. D. McClatchy. Used by permission of Alfred A. Knopf, a division of Random House, Inc.

Sandra McPherson: "The Ability to Make a Face like a Spider While Singing

Naomi Shihab Nye: "Violin" from *Red Suitcase*. Copyright © 1994 by Naomi Shihab Nye. Reprinted with the permission of BOA Editions, Ltd.

Frank O'Hara: "On Rachmaninoff's Birthday" from *Lunch Poems* (City Lights, 1964). © 1964 by Frank O'Hara. Reprinted by pemission of City Lights Books.

Mary Oliver: "Mozart, For Example" from *Thirst* by Mary Oliver. Copyright © 2006 by Mary Oliver. Reprinted by permission of Beacon Press, Boston. "Such Singing in the Wild Branches" from *Owls and Other Fantasies* by Mary Oliver. Copyright © 2003 by Mary Oliver. Reprinted by permission of Beacon Press, Boston.

Gregory Orr: "His song was about the world" from *Concerning the Book that is the Body of the Beloved*. Copyright © 2006 by Gregory Orr. Reprinted with the permission of Copper Canyon Press, www.coppercanyonpress.org.

Linda Pastan: "Practicing," "Muse" from *The Last Uncle* by Linda Pastan. Copyright © 2002 by Linda Pastan. Used by permission of W. W. Norton & Company, Inc. "Beethoven's Quartet in C Major, Opus 59" from *Queen of Rainy Country* by Linda Pastan. Copyright © 2006 by Linda Pastan. Used by permission of W.W. Norton & Company, Inc.

Nils Peterson: "For Charlene" appeared originally in *Caesura*. Copyright © by Nils Peterson. Used by kind permission of the author.

Robert Phillips: "Instrument of Choice" from *Spinach Days* (Johns Hopkins University Press). Copyright © 2000 by Robert Phillips. Reprinted by kind permission of the author.

Robert Pinsky: "Ginza Samba" from *The Figured Wheel: New and Collected Poems 1966–1996* by Robert Pinsky. Copyright © 1996 by Robert Pinsky. Reprinted by permission of Farrar, Straus and Giroux. LLC.

Vasko Popa: "The Blackbird's Song" from *Vasko Popa: Collected Poems*. Translation copyright © 1978 by Anne Remington. Reprinted by permission of Persea Books.

Ann Porter: "Music" from *Living Things: Collected Poems* (Zoland Books, 2006). Copyright © by Anne Porter 2006. Reprinted by permission of Steerforth Press.

Carl Rakosi: "Instructions to a Player" in *The Collected Poems of Carl Rakosi*, published by The National Poetry Foundation, University of Maine, Orono, Maine. By kind permission of the executor, Marilyn J. Kane.

Liam Rector: "The Eventual Music" from *American Prodigal*, published by Story Line. Copyright © 1994 by Liam Rector. Used by kind permission of the author.

Rumi: "Where Everything Is Music" from *The Essential Rumi*, 1995, translated by Coleman Barks. Copyright © by Coleman Barks. By kind permission of the translator.

Muriel Rukeyser: "Gradus Ad Parnassum" from *A Muriel Rukeyser Reader*. New York: W. W. Norton & Company, 1994. Copyright © 1994 by Muriel